LEARN FRENCH WITH FAII

ISBN: 978-1-987949-97-1

This book is published by Bermuda Word. It has been created with specialized software that produces a three line interlinear format.

Please contact us if you would like a pdf version of this book with different font, font size, or font colors and/or less words per page!

LEARN-TO-READ-FOREIGN-LANGUAGES.COM

BER**⋂**UDA
ⵑ**⋃**ORD

Dear Reader and Language Learner!

You're reading the Paperback edition of Bermuda Word's interlinear and pop-up HypLern Reader App. Before you start reading French, please read this explanation of our method.

Since we want you to read French and to learn French, our method consists primarily of word-for-word literal translations, but we add idiomatic English if this helps understanding the sentence.

For example:
Il y   avait du   vin
It there had of the wine
[There was wine]

The HypLern method entails that you re-read the text until you know the high frequency words just by reading, and then mark and learn the low frequency words in your reader or practice them with our brilliant App.

Don't forget to take a look at the e-book App with integrated learning software that we offer at learn-to-read-foreign-languages.com! For more info check the last two pages of this e-book!

Thanks for your patience and enjoy the story and learning French!

Kees van den End

LEARN-TO-READ-FOREIGN-LANGUAGES.COM

TABLE   DES   MATIÈRES
TABLE   OF THE CONTENTS
             (OF)

LES TROIS OURS
THE THREE BEARS

Il y avait une fois un, deux, trois ours: Papa ours,
It there had   one   time   one   two   three   bears   Papa   bear
(There were)

Maman ours, et Petit ours.
Mama   bear   and Little bear

Les trois ours demeuraient dans une petite maison,
The   three bears stayed   in   a   small   house
                    (lived)

dans une grande forêt.
in   a   large   forest

Dans la maison, il y avait trois lits: un grand lit pour
In   the house   it there had three beds one large bed for
                   (there were)

Papa ours, un lit moyen pour Maman ours, et un
Papa   bear   one bed middle-sized for Mama   bear   and one

petit lit pour Petit ours.
small bed for   Little bear

Il y avait aussi trois chaises: une grande chaise pour
It there had   also   three   chairs   one   large   chair   for
(There were)

Papa ours, une chaise moyenne pour Maman ours, et
Papa   bear   a   chair   middle-sized   for   Mama   bear   and

une petite chaise pour Petit ours.
one   small   chair   for   Little   bear

Il y avait aussi trois assiettes et trois cuillères: une
It there had   also   three   plates   and   three   spoons   one
(There were)

grande assiette et une grande cuillère pour Papa ours,
large   plate   and one   large   spoon   for   Papa   bear

une assiette moyenne et une cuillère moyenne pour
one   plate   middle-sized   and one   spoon   middle-sized   for

Maman ours, et une petite assiette et une petite
Mama   bear   and one   small   plate   and one   small

cuillère pour Petit ours.
spoon   for   Little   bear

7 Les Trois Ours

Un jour Papa ours dit de sa grande voix: "J'ai faim."
One day Papa bear said of his great voice I have hunger
(with) (loud) (am) (hungry)

"Oui," dit Maman ours de sa voix moyenne, "J'ai
Yes said Mama bear of her voice average I have
(with) (am)

faim." Et Petit ours dit de sa petite voix: "Oui, oui,
hunger And Little bear said of his little voice Yes yes
(hungry) (with) (soft)

j'ai faim."
I have hunger
(am) (hungry)

Verser

Les trois ours firent la soupe. Alors ils versèrent la
The three bears made the soup Then they poured the

soupe dans les trois assiettes. Ils versèrent une grande
soup in the three plates They poured one large

portion dans la grande assiette pour Papa ours.
portion in the large plate for Papa bear

Ils versèrent une portion moyenne dans l'assiette de
They poured one portion middle-sized in the plate of

Maman ours, et une petite portion dans la petite
Mama bear and one small portion in the small

assiette de Petit ours.
plate of Little bear

Alors Papa ours prit la grande cuillère, goûta la
Then Papa bear took the large spoon tasted the

soupe et dit: "La soupe est trop chaude." Maman
soup and said The soup is too hot Mama

ours prit la cuillère moyenne, goûta la soupe et dit:
bear took the spoon middle-sized tasted the soup and said

"Oui, la soupe est trop chaude," et Petit ours prit la
Yes the soup is too hot and Little bear took the

petite cuillère, goûta la soupe et dit: "Oui, oui, la
small spoon tasted the soup and said Yes yes the

soupe est trop chaude."
soup is too hot

9 Les Trois Ours

Alors Papa ours dit: "Allons nous promener dans la
Then Papa bear said Let us go walk in the

forêt." "Oui," dit Maman ours, "allons nous promener
forest Yes said Mama bear let us go walk

dans la forêt ;" et Petit ours dit: "Oui, oui,
in the forest and Little bear said Yes yes

allons nous promener dans la forêt."
let us go walk in the forest

Les trois ours partirent. Ils laissèrent la porte de la
The three bears left They left the door of the

maison ouverte, et la soupe sur la table. Une petite
house opened and the soup on the table One little

fille passa. Elle vit la petite maison, elle vit la porte
girl passed She saw the small house she saw the door

ouverte, et elle vit la soupe sur la table. Elle dit:
opened and she saw the soup on the table She said

"J'ai faim," et elle entra dans la maison.
I have hunger and she entered in the house
(I am) (hungry)

Elle   prit   la   grande   cuillère,   goûta   la   soupe   dans   la
She   took   the large   spoon   tasted the soup   in   the

grande   assiette,   et   dit: "Cette   soupe   est   trop   chaude."
large   plate   and said   This   soup   is   too   hot

Alors   elle   prit   la   cuillère   moyenne,   goûta   la   soupe
Then   she   took   the spoon   middle-sized tasted the soup

dans   l'assiette   moyenne,   et   dit: "Cette   soupe   est   trop
in   the plate   middle-sized and said   This   soup   is   too

froide."   Alors   elle   prit   la   petite   cuillère,   goûta   la   soupe
cold   Then   she   took   the small   spoon   tasted the soup

dans   la   petite   assiette,   et   dit: "Cette   soupe   est
in   the small   plate   and said   This   soup   is

excellente."   La   petite   fille   mangea   toute   la   soupe.
excellent   The little   girl   ate   all   the soup

Alors   la   petite   fille   dit: "Je   suis   fatiguée,   où   y   a-t-il
Then   the little   girl   said   I   am   tired   where there has it
                                                                     (is)

une   chaise?"
a   chair

11   Les Trois Ours

Elle (She) vit (saw) les (the) trois (three) chaises. (chairs) Elle (She) alla (went) à (to) la (the) grande (large)

chaise, (chair) s'assit, (sat down) et (and) dit: (said) "Cette (This) chaise (chair) n'est pas (is not)

confortable." (comfortable) Elle (She) alla (went) à (to) la (the) chaise (chair) moyenne, (middle-sized) s'assit, (sat down) et (and)

dit: (said) "Cette (This) chaise (chair) n'est pas (is not) confortable." (comfortable) Alors (Then) elle (she) alla (went)

à (to) la (the) petite (small) chaise, (chair) s'assit, (sat down) et (and) dit: (said) "Cette (This) chaise (chair) est (is)

très (very) confortable." (comfortable) Alors (Then) la (the) petite (little) fille (girl) sauta (jumped) de (of) joie (joy) et (and)

la (the) chaise (chair) se cassa! (broke)

La (The) petite (little) fille (girl) dit: (said) "J'ai (I have) (I am) sommeil, (sleep) (sleepy) où (where) y (there has it) a-t-il (is there) un (a) lit?" (bed)

Elle (She) vit (saw) les (the) trois (three) lits. (beds) Elle (She) alla (went) au (to the) grand (large) lit, (bed)

se coucha, (laid down) et (and) dit: (said) "Ce (This) lit (bed) n'est pas (is not) confortable." (comfortable)

Elle alla au lit moyen, se coucha, et dit: "Ce lit
She went to the bed middle-sized laid down and said This bed

n'est pas confortable." Alors elle alla au petit lit,
is not comfortable Then she went to the small bed

se coucha, et dit: "Ce lit est très confortable," et la
laid down and said This bed is very comfortable and the

petite fille s'endormit.
little girl fell asleep

Vingt minutes après les trois ours arrivèrent. Papa ours
Twenty minutes later the three bears arrived Papa bear

regarda sa grande cuillère et sa grande assiette, et
looked at his large spoon and his large plate and

dit de sa grande voix: "Quelqu'un est entré et a
said of his great voice Somebody is entered and has
(with) (has)

goûté ma soupe." Maman ours regarda sa cuillère et
tasted my soup Mama bear looked at her spoon and

son assiette, et dit:
her plate and said

"Oui, quelqu'un est entré et a goûté ma soupe," et
Yes somebody is entered and has tasted my soup   and
(has)

Petit ours regarda sa petite cuillère et sa petite
Little bear looked at his small spoon and his small

assiette, et dit de sa petite voix: "Oui, oui, quelqu'un
plate   and said of his little voice: Yes yes somebody
(with)

est entré et a mangé toute ma soupe."
is entered and has eaten all my soup
(has entered)

Papa ours regarda sa grande chaise et dit de sa
Papa bear looked at his large chair and said of his
(with)

grande voix: "Quelqu'un est entré et s'est assis sur
great voice Somebody is entered and is sat on
(loud)   (has)   (has)   (in)

ma chaise." Maman ours regarda sa chaise, et dit:
my chair   Mama bear looked at her chair and said

"Oui, quelqu'un est entré et s'est assis sur ma
Yes somebody is entered and is sat on my
(has)   (has)

chaise."
chair

Et   Petit   ours   regarda   sa   petite   chaise,   et   dit   de   sa
And Little bear   looked at his small   chair   and said of   his
                                                                      (with)

petite   voix: "Oui,   oui,   quelqu'un   est   entré   et   a   cassé
little   voice   Yes   yes   somebody   is   entered and has broken
(soft)

ma   petite   chaise."
my   small   chair

Alors   Papa   ours   regarda   son   grand   lit   et   dit   de   sa
Then   Papa   bear   looked at his   large   bed   and said of   his
                                                                     (with)

grande   voix: "Quelqu'un   est   entré   et   s'est   couché   sur
great   voice   Somebody   is   entered   and is   slept   on
(loud)   (has)   (has)

mon   grand   lit."   Maman   ours   regarda   son   lit,   et   dit:
my   large   bed   Mama   bear   looked at her   bed   and said

"Oui,   quelqu'un   est   entré   et   s'est   couché   sur   mon   lit."
Yes   somebody   is   entered   and is   slept   on   my   bed
                    (has)   (has)

Et   Petit   ours   regarda   son   petit   lit,   et   dit   de   sa
And Little bear   looked at his   small   bed   and said of   his
                                                                    (with)

petite   voix:
little   voice

"Oui, oui, une petite fille est couchée sur mon petit
Yes yes a   little girl is lying   on my little

lit."
bed

Les trois ours s'approchèrent: "Oh!" dit Papa ours,
The three bears approached   Oh   said Papa bear

"cette petite fille est jolie." Maman ours dit: "Oh, oui,
this little girl is pretty Mama bear said Oh yes

cette petite fille est jolie," et le petit ours dit: "Oh!
this little girl is pretty, and the little bear said Oh

oui, oui, cette petite fille est très jolie."
yes yes this little girl is very pretty

A cet instant la petite fille se réveilla. Elle vit Papa
At this moment the small girl awoke   She saw Papa

ours, Maman ours, et Petit ours. Elle dit: "Oh! J'ai
bear Mama bear, and Little bear. She said Oh I have
                                                  (I am)

peur," et elle sauta du lit et partit vite, vite!
fear and she jumped from the bed and got out quickly quickly
(afraid)

"Oh!"　dit　Papa　ours　de　sa　grande　voix:　"La　petite
Oh　　said　Papa　bear　of　his　great　voice　The　little
　　　　　　　　　　　　　　　(with)　(loud)

fille　a　peur."　"Oui,"　dit　Maman　ours,　"la　petite　fille　a
girl　has　fear　Yes　said　Mama　bear　the　little　girl　has
　　(is)　(afraid)　　　　　　　　　　　　　　　　　　(is)

peur."　Et　le　petit　ours　dit:　"Oui,　oui,　elle　a　peur."
fear　And　the　small　bear　said　Yes　yes　she　has　fear
(afraid)　　　　　　　　　　　　　　　　　　(is)　(afraid)

La　petite　fille　ne　visita　plus　jamais　la　maison　des
The　little　girl　not　visited　more　never　the　house　of the
　　　　　　　　　　　(anymore)

ours.
bears

17   Les Trois Ours

LES   TROIS   SOUHAITS
THE   THREE   WISHES

Il y avait une fois un homme qui était très pauvre. Il
It there had   one   time   a   man   who was   very   poor   He
(There was)

demeurait avec sa femme dans une misérable petite
resided   with   his   wife   in   a   wretched   little
(lived)

maison. Tous les jours l'homme allait à la forêt pour
house   All   the   days   the man   went   to the forest   to

couper du bois. Un jour il était dans la forêt et dit:
cut   of the wood   One   day   he   was   in   the forest and said
()

"Je suis bien misérable! Je suis pauvre, je suis forcé
I   am   very   miserable   I   am   poor   I   am   forced

de travailler tous les jours. Ma femme a faim, j'ai
to   work   all   the   days   My   wife   has hunger   I have
                                                   (is) (hungry) (I am)

faim aussi. Oui, je suis bien misérable!"
hunger also   Yes   I   am   very   miserable
(hungry)

A cet instant une jolie petite fée parut, et dit:
At   this   moment   a   cute   little   fairy appeared and said

"Mon pauvre homme, j'ai entendu tout ce que vous
My poor man I have heard all this that you

avez dit. J'ai compassion de vous, et comme je suis
have said I have pity of you, and as I am
(with)

fée je vous accorderai trois souhaits. Demandez ce
fairy I you will grant three wishes. Ask that

que vous voulez, et vos trois souhaits seront
what you want and your three wishes will be

accordés."
granted

La fée disparut après avoir parlé ainsi, et le pauvre
The fairy disappeared after to have spoken thus, and the poor

homme resta tout seul dans la forêt.
man remained all alone in the forest.

Il était très content maintenant, et dit: "Je vais à la
He was very satisfied now, and said I go to the

maison. Je vais dire à ma femme qu'une fée m'a
house I go say to my wife that a fairy me has

accordé trois souhaits."
granted three wishes.

21 Les Trois Souhaits

Le pauvre homme alla à la maison, et dit à sa
The poor man went to the house and said to his

femme: "Ma femme, je suis très content. J'ai vu une
wife My woman I am very satisfied I have seen a
(met)

fée dans la forêt. La fée a dit: 'Mon pauvre homme,
fairy in the forest The fairy has said My poor man

j'ai compassion de vous. Je suis fée, et je vous
I have pity of you I am fairy and I you
(for)

accorderai trois souhaits. Demandez ce que vous
will grant three wishes Ask that what you

voulez.' Ma femme, je suis très content."
want My wife I am very satisfied

"Oh oui," dit la pauvre femme, "je suis très contente
Oh yes said the poor woman I am very satisfied

aussi. Entrez dans la maison, mon cher ami, et nous
also Enter inside the house my dear friend and we

parlerons ensemble de la fée et des trois souhaits."
will speak together of the fairy and of the three wishes

"Certainement,"   dit   l'homme.   Il   entra   dans   la   maison,
Certainly   said   the man   He   entered   in   the   house

s'assit   près   de   la   table,   et   dit: "Ma   femme,   j'ai   faim.
sat down   near of   the   table   and   said   My   wife   I have hunger
           (at)   (I am) (hungry)

Je   propose   de   dîner.   Pendant   le   dîner   nous   parlerons
I   propose   to   dine   During   the   dinner   we   will speak

ensemble   de   la   fée   et   des   trois   souhaits."
together   about the   fairy and   of the three   wishes

Le   pauvre   homme   et   la   pauvre   femme   s'assirent
The   poor   man   and   the   poor   woman   sat down

près   de   la   table   et   commencèrent   à   manger   et   à
near of   the   table   and   began   to   eat   and   to
(at)

parler   ensemble.   Le   pauvre   homme   dit: "Ma   femme,
speak   together   The   poor   man   said   My   woman

nous   pouvons   demander   de   grandes   richesses."   "Oui,"
we   can   ask   of   great   fortunes   Yes
                                ()

dit   la   femme,   "nous   pouvons   demander   une   jolie
said   the   woman   we   can   ask   a   pretty

maison."   L'homme   dit:
house   The man   said

"Nous   pouvons   demander   un   empire."   La   femme
We   can   ask   an   empire   The   woman

répondit: "Oui,   nous   pouvons   demander   des   perles   et
answered   Yes   we   can   ask   of the pearls   and
                                                     ()

des   diamants   en   grande   quantité."
of the   diamonds   in   large   quantity
()

L'homme   dit: "Nous   pouvons   demander   une   grande
The man   said   We   can   ask   a   large

famille,   cinq   fils   et   cinq   filles."
family   five   sons   and   five   daughters

"Oh,"   dit   la   femme,   "je   préfère   six   fils   et   quatre
Oh   said   the   woman   I   prefer   six   sons   and   four

filles."
girls

L'homme   et   la   femme   continuèrent   ainsi,   leur
The man   and   the   woman   continued   this way   their

conversation,   mais   ils   ne   pouvaient   pas   décider   quels
conversation   but   they   not   could   not   decide   what
                                          ()

souhaits   seraient   les   plus   sages.
wishes   would be   the   most   wise

L'homme mangea sa soupe en silence regarda le pain
The man   ate   his soup in silence looked at the bread

sec, et dit: "Oh! j'aimerais avoir une bonne grosse
dry and said Oh I would like to have one good big

saucisse pour dîner." Au même instant une grosse
sausage to   dine   At the same moment a   big

saucisse tomba sur la table. L'homme regarda la
sausage fell on the table. The man looked at the

saucisse avec la plus grande surprise, la femme aussi.
sausage with the greatest surprise the woman also

Alors la femme dit: "Oh, mon mari, vous avez été
Then the woman said Oh my husband you have been

très imprudent. Vous avez demandé une saucisse
very careless   You have asked a   sausage

seulement. Un souhait est accordé. Maintenant il reste
only   One wish   is granted   Now   it remain
                                                  (there)

seulement deux souhaits." "Oui," dit l'homme, "j'ai été
only   two wishes   Yes said the man   I have been

imprudent, mais il y a encore deux souhaits."
careless   but it there has still two wishes
                it there has still
                (there are still)

"Nous pouvons demander de grandes richesses et un
We can ask of large fortunes and an
()

empire." "Oui," dit la femme, "nous pouvons demander
empire Yes said the woman we can ask

encore de grandes richesses et un empire, mais nous
still of great fortunes and an empire but we
()

ne pouvons pas demander dix enfants. Vous avez été
not can not ask ten children You have been
()

si imprudent. Vous avez demandé une saucisse. Vous
so careless You have asked a sausage You

préférez une saucisse, sans doute, à une grande
prefer a sausage without doubt to a large

famille." Et la pauvre femme continua ses lamentations
family And the poor woman continued her lamentations

et répéta si souvent: "Vous avez été très imprudent,"
and repeated so often You have been very careless

que l'homme perdit patience et dit: "Je suis fatigué de
that the man lost patience and said I am tired of

vos lamentations: je voudrais que cette saucisse fût
your lamentations I would like that this sausage was

pendue au bout de votre nez!"
hung at the end of your nose

Un instant après la saucisse était pendue au bout du
One moment afterwards the sausage was hung at the end of the

nez de la pauvre femme. La pauvre femme était très
nose of the poor woman. The poor woman was very

surprise, et l'homme aussi. La femme commença à
surprised, and the man also. The woman started to

se lamenter encore plus, et dit à son mari: "Ah, mon
to deplore herself still more, and said to her husband Ah, my

mari, vous êtes bien imprudent. Vous avez demandé
husband you are very careless. You have asked

une saucisse, et maintenant vous avez demandé que
a sausage, and now you have asked that

cette saucisse fût pendue au bout de mon nez. C'est
this sausage was hung at the end of my nose. It is
(should be)

terrible. Deux souhaits sont accordés. Maintenant il reste
terrible. Two wishes are granted Now it remains
(there)

seulement un souhait!"
only one wish

"Oui," dit l'homme. "Mais nous pouvons demander de
Yes said the man But we can ask of
()

grandes richesses."
great fortunes

"Oui," dit la femme, "mais j'ai une saucisse pendue
Yes said the woman but I have a sausage hung

au bout du nez. Je suis ridicule. J'étais jolie,
at the end of the nose I am ridiculous I was pretty

maintenant je suis laide, et c'est de votre faute!" et
now I am ugly and it is of your fault and
(because of)

la pauvre femme pleura.
the poor woman cried

L'homme regarda sa femme, et dit: "Oh, j'aimerais que
The man looked at his woman and said Oh I would like that

cette saucisse ne fût pas ici." À l'instant la saucisse
that sausage not was not here At the instant the sausage
()

disparut, et l'homme et la femme étaient aussi pauvres
disappeared and the man and the woman were as poor

qu'avant. La femme se lamenta, l'homme aussi, mais
as before The woman herself deplored the man also but
(was complaining)

les trois souhaits avaient été accordés, et l'homme
the three wishes had been granted and the man

se trouva obligé de manger son pain sec.
himself found obliged to eat his bread dry

Après   le   dîner   il   retourna   à   la   forêt   pour   couper   du
After   the   dinner   he   returned   to   the   forest   to   cut   of the
()

bois.   Il   dit: "Je   suis   bien   bien   misérable,"   mais   la
wood   He   said   I   am   very   very   miserable   but   the

fée   n'arriva pas,   et   il   resta   toujours   pauvre.
fairy   not arrived not   and   he   remained   always   poor
        (did not arrive)

Il   n'avait pas   de   richesses,   il   n'avait pas   d'empire,   il
He   not had not   of the   fortunes   he   not had not   of empire   he
        (did not have)   ()   (did not have)   (an empire)

n'avait pas   de   perles,   il   n'avait pas   de   diamants,   il
not had not   of   pearls   he   not had not   of   diamonds   he
(did not have)   ()   (did not have)   ()

n'avait pas   de   fils,   il   n'avait pas   de   filles,   et   il
not had not   of   sons   he   not had not   of   daughters   and   he
(did not have)   ()   (did not have)   ()

n'avait pas   même   une   saucisse   pour   son   dîner.
not had not   even   a   sausage   for   his   dinner
(did not have)

Sa   femme   continua   à   pleurer,   et   elle   disait   tous   les
His   wife   continued   to   cry   and   she   said   all   the

jours   à   son   mari:
days   to   her   husband

"Ah,   si   vous   n'aviez   pas   été   si   imprudent,   nous
Ah   if   you   not had not   been   so   careless   we
                  (had not)

serions   riches   et   contents,   et   nous   aurions   une   grande
would be   rich   and satisfied   and   we   would have   a   large

famille.   Hélas!   hélas!"
family   Alas   alas

BLANCHE-NEIGE
WHITE-SNOW
(SNOW WHITE)

Il   y   avait   un   paysan   appelé   Ivan,   sa   femme
It there had   a   peasant   called   Ivan   his   wife
(There was)

se   nommait   Marie.   Ces   paysans   n'avaient   pas   d'enfants,
herself named Marie   These   peasants   not had not   of children
(was called)   (did not have)   (children)

et   ils   étaient   très   tristes.
and   they   were   very   sad

Un   jour,   en   hiver,   le   paysan   était   assis   à   la   fenêtre.
One   day   in   winter   the   peasant   was   seated   at   the   window
                                                         (sitting)

Il   vit   les   enfants   du   village   qui   jouaient   dans   la
He   saw   the   children   of the   village   who   played   in   the

neige.   Les   enfants   étaient   très   occupés.   Ils   faisaient
snow   The   children   were   very   busy   They   made

une   bonne   femme   de   neige.
a   nice   woman   of   snow

Ivan dit à sa femme: "Ma femme, regardez ces
Ivan said to his wife My wife look at these

enfants, ils s'amusent, ils font une bonne femme de
children they amuse themselves they make a nice woman of

neige. Venez dans le jardin, amusons-nous à faire une
snow Come into the garden let us amuse ourselves by making a

bonne femme de neige." Le paysan et sa femme
nice woman of snow The peasant and his wife

allèrent dans le jardin, et la femme dit: "Mon mari,
went into the garden and the woman said My husband

nous n'avons pas d'enfants; faisons un enfant de
we do not have of children let us make a child of
(children)

neige."
snow

"Voilà une bonne idée!" dit l'homme. Et il commença
See there a good idea said the man And he started
(That is)

à façonner un petit corps, de petites mains, de petits
to fashion a small body of small hands of small
(with) (with)

pieds. La femme façonna une petite tête et la plaça
feet The woman fashioned a small head and it placed

sur les épaules de la statue de neige.
on the shoulders of the statue of snow

Un homme passait sur la route; il les regarda un
A man passed on the road he them looked at one

instant en silence, puis il dit: "Dieu vous aide."
moment in silence then he said God you help

"Merci," dit Ivan.
Thank you said Ivan

"Le secours de Dieu est toujours bon à
The help of God is always good for

quelque chose," répondit Marie.
something answered Marie

"Que faites-vous donc?" demanda le passant.
What make you then asked the passer by

"Nous faisons une fille de neige," dit Ivan. Et en
We make a girl of snow said Ivan And in

parlant ainsi il fit le nez, le menton, la bouche et
speaking thus he made the nose the chin the mouth and

les yeux. En quelques minutes l'enfant de neige était
the eyes In some minutes the child of snow was
(a few)

finie.
finished

Ivan la regarda avec admiration. Tout à coup il
Ivan her looked at with admiration All at strike (once) he

remarqua que la bouche et les yeux s'ouvraient. Les
noted that the mouth and the eyes opened The

joues et les lèvres changèrent de couleur, et quelques
cheeks and the lips changed of color and some
()

minutes après il vit devant lui une enfant vivante.
minutes afterwards he saw in front of him a child alive

"Qui êtes-vous?" dit-il tout surpris de voir une enfant
Who are you said he all surprised of to see a child

vivante à la place de la petite statue de neige.
alive in the place of the small statue of snow

"Je suis Blanche-Neige, votre fille," dit l'enfant, et elle
I am White Snow your daughter said the child and she

embrassa l'homme et la femme, qui commencèrent à
embraced the man and the woman who began to

pleurer de joie.
cry of joy

35 Blanche Neige

Les parents conduisirent Blanche-Neige dans la maison,
The parents led White Snow in the house

et elle commença à grandir très rapidement.
and she started to grow very quickly

Toutes les petites filles du village arrivèrent chez le
All the little girls of the village arrived at the

paysan pour jouer avec la charmante petite fille. Elle
peasant to play with the charming little girl She
(peasant's house)

était si bonne et si jolie. Elle était blanche comme
was so good and so pretty She was white like

la neige, elle avait les yeux bleus comme le ciel, sa
the snow she had the eyes blue like the sky her

longue chevelure dorée était admirable, et bien que ses
long hair golden was admirable and although her

joues ne fussent pas aussi roses que celles des autres
cheeks were not so pink as those of the other

enfants du village, elle était si douce que tout le
children of the village she was so soft that all the

monde l'aimait beaucoup.
world her liked much

L'hiver   se   passa   très   rapidement,   et   Blanche-Neige
The winter   passed   very   quickly   and   White Snow

grandit   si   vite   que   quand   le   soleil   du   printemps
grew   so   quickly   that   when   the   sun   of the   spring

fit   verdir   l'herbe,   elle   était   aussi   grande   qu'une   fille   de
made   become green   the grass   she   was   as   large   as a   girl   of

douze   ou   treize   ans.   Pendant   l'hiver   Blanche-Neige   avait
twelve   or   thirteen   years   During   the winter   White Snow   had

toujours   été   très   gaie,   mais   quand   le   beau   temps
always   been   very   merry   but   when   the   beautiful   weather

arriva   elle   était   toute   triste.   La   mère   Marie   remarqua
arrived   she   was   all   sad   The   mother   Marie   noted

sa   tristesse,   et   dit: "Ma   chère   enfant,   pourquoi
her   sadness   and   said   My   dear   child   why

êtes-vous   triste?   Êtes-vous   malade?"   "Non,   je
are you   sad   Are you   ill   No   I

ne   suis   pas   malade,   ma   bonne   mère,"   répondit   l'enfant,
am not   ill   my   good   mother   answered   the child

et   elle   resta   tranquille   dans   la   maison.
and   she   remained   quiet   in   the   house

37 Blanche Neige

Les	petites	filles	du	village	arrivèrent	et	dirent:
The	small	girls	of the	village	arrived	and	said

"Blanche-Neige,	venez	avec	nous,	venez	avec	nous,
White Snow	come	with	us	come	with	us

nous	allons	au	bois	cueillir	des	fleurs."
we	go	to the	forest	to gather	of the ()	flowers

"Voilà	une	bonne	idée!"	dit	Marie.	"Allez	au	bois	avec
See there	a	good	idea	said	Marie	Go	to the	forest	with

vos	petites	amies,	mon	enfant,	allez	et	amusez-vous
your	little	friends	my	child	go	and	amuse yourself

bien!"
well

Les	enfants	partirent.	Elles	allèrent	au	bois,	elles
The	children	left	They	went	to the	forest	they

cueillirent	des	fleurs,	elles	firent	des	bouquets	et	des
gathered	of the ()	flowers	they	made	of the ()	bouquets	and	of the ()

couronnes,	et	quand	le	soir	arriva	elles	firent	un
crowns	and	when	the	evening	arrived	they	made	a

grand	feu.
large	fire

"Maintenant, Blanche-Neige, regardez bien et faites
Now White Snow look well and do

comme nous," dirent-elles, et elles commencèrent à
like us said they and they began to

chanter et à danser. Elles sautèrent aussi l'une après
sing and to dance They jumped also the one after

l'autre à travers le feu. Tout à coup elles entendirent
the other through the fire Suddenly they heard

une exclamation: "Ah!" Toutes les petites filles
an exclamation Ah All the little girls

regardèrent, et un instant après elles remarquèrent que
watched and one moment after they noted that

Blanche-Neige n'était plus là.
White Snow was not more there
(anymore)

"Blanche-Neige, où êtes-vous?" crièrent-elles, mais
White Snow where are you shouted they but

Blanche-Neige ne répondit pas. Les petites filles
White Snow not answered The little girls

cherchèrent en vain, elles ne trouvèrent pas leur petite
sought in vain they found not their little

compagne.
friend

Ivan,	Marie	et	tous	les	paysans	cherchèrent	aussi	en
Ivan	Marie	and	all	the	peasants	sought	also	in

vain,	car	la	petite	Blanche-Neige	s'était	changée	en
vain	because	the	little	White Snow	was	herself changed (was changed)	in

une	petite	vapeur	au	contact	du	feu,	et	elle	s'était
a	small (bit of)	vapor	at the	contact	of the (with the)	fire	and	she	was

envolée	vers	le	ciel	d'où	elle	était	venue	sous	la
in flight	towards	the	sky	from where	she	was (had)	arrival (come)	under (in)	the

forme	d'un	flocon	de	neige.
form	of a	flake	of	snow

LA ROSE MOUSSEUSE
THE ROSE MOSSY

L'Amour alla un jour se promener dans la forêt. C'était
The Love went one day to walk in the forest It was
(Cupid)

un beau jour au mois de Juin. L'Amour se promena
a beautiful day in the month of June The Love walked
(Cupid)

longtemps, longtemps. Il se promena si longtemps qu'il
long time long time He walked so long that he
(a long time) (a long time)

se trouva enfin fatigué, bien fatigué.
himself found finally tired well tired
(became)

"Oh!" dit L'Amour, "je suis si fatigué!" Et L'Amour
Oh said The Love I am so tired And The Love
(Cupid) (Cupid)

se coucha sur l'herbe verte pour se reposer. Tous les
laid down on the grass green for to rest himself All the

petits oiseaux de la forêt arrivèrent vite, vite pour voir
little birds of the forest arrived quickly quickly for to see

l'Amour.
The Love
(Cupid)

L'Amour était si joli, si blanc et rose. L'Amour avait
Cupid was so pretty so white and pink Cupid had

de si jolis cheveux blonds et de si jolis yeux bleus.
of such pretty hairs fair and of such pretty eyes blue
()   ()

"Oh!" dirent tous les petits oiseaux de la forêt.
Oh said all the little birds of the forest

"Regardez le petit Amour! Comme il est joli! Comme
Look at the little Cupid How he is pretty How

il est blanc et rose! Quel joli Amour! Quels jolis
he is white and pink What pretty Cupid What pretty
                              (What a)

cheveux blonds! Quels jolis yeux bleus!"
hair fair What pretty eyes blue

Tous les oiseaux se perchèrent sur les branches et
All the birds perched themselves on the branches and

commencèrent à chanter en choeur: "Quel joli petit
began to sing in chorus What pretty little

Amour!"
Cupid

43   La Rose Mousseuse

Le petit Amour ferma ses jolis yeux bleus.
The little Cupid closed his pretty eyes blue

Le petit Amour s'endormit. Il s'endormit profondément.
The little Cupid fell asleep He fell asleep deeply

Les petits oiseaux continuèrent à chanter, "Quel joli
The little birds continued to sing What pretty
(What a)

petit Amour!"
little Cupid

Alors le Soleil dit: "Les petits oiseaux de la forêt
Then the Sun said The little birds of the forest

chantent tous: 'Quel joli petit Amour!' Où est ce joli
sing all What pretty little Cupid Where is this pretty
(What a)

petit Amour?" et le Soleil entra dans la forêt pour
little Cupid and the Sun entered into the forest for

chercher le joli petit Amour.
to seek the pretty little Cupid

Le   Soleil   entra   dans   la   forêt,   et,   guidé   par   le   chant
The   Sun   entered   into   the   forest   and   guided   by   the   song

des   petits   oiseaux,   il   arriva   bientôt   à   la   place   où   le
of the   little   birds   he   arrived   soon   at   the   place   where   the

joli   petit   Amour   était   couché   sur   l'herbe   verte.
pretty   little   Cupid   was   lying down   on   the grass   green

"Oh!"   dit   le   Soleil,   "Quel   joli   petit   Amour!   Comme   il
Oh   said   the   Sun   What   pretty   little   Cupid   How   he
(What a)

est   blanc   et   rose!   Quels   jolis   cheveux   blonds!   Quelle
is   white   and   pink   What   pretty   hair   fair   What

est   la   couleur   des   yeux   de   ce   joli   petit   Amour?"
is   the   color   of the   eyes   of   this   pretty   little   Cupid

Le   Soleil   était   curieux,   très   curieux,   mais   la   Rose   qui
The   Sun   was   curious   very   curious   but   the   Rose   who

était   là   dit: "Non,   non,   Soleil,   vous   êtes   curieux,   très
was   there   said   No   no   Sun   you   are   curious   very

curieux,   mais   le   joli   petit   Amour   dort."
curious   but   the   pretty   little   Cupid   sleeps

Partez,   méchant   Soleil,   partez   vite.   L'Amour   dort
Leave   mean   Sun   leave   quickly Cupid   sleeps

profondément,   et   les   petits   oiseaux   chantent.   Partez!
deeply   and the   little   birds   sing   Leave

"Oh   non!"   dit   le   Soleil.   "Je   veux   voir   quelle   est   la
Oh   no   said the Sun   I   want   to see what   is   the

couleur   des   yeux   de   ce   joli   petit   Amour."
color   of the eyes   of   this pretty little   Cupid

"Non,   non!"   dit   la   Rose,   et   elle   se   pencha   sur
No   no   said the Rose   and she   herself leaned over

L'Amour,   et   elle   le   protégea.   La   Rose   protégea   le
Cupid   and she   him protected   The Rose   protected the

petit   Amour,   et   le   Soleil,   le   Soleil   curieux,   resta   dans
little   Cupid   and the Sun   the Sun   curious   remained in

la   forêt,   et   dit:
the forest   and said

"Je   veux   voir   la   couleur   des   yeux   de   ce   joli   petit
I   want   to see the color   of the eyes   of   this pretty little

Amour."
Cupid

"Je resterai ici, dans la forêt, et quand l'Amour
I   will remain   here   in   the   forest   and   when   Cupid

ouvrira les yeux, je serai content, très content."
will open   the   eyes   I   will be   satisfied   very   satisfied

Le Soleil resta dans la forêt, les oiseaux chantèrent,
The   Sun   remained   in   the   forest   the   birds   sang

la Rose protégea l'Amour, et l'Amour dormit profondément.
the   Rose   protected   Cupid   and   Cupid   slept   deeply

Enfin l'Amour ouvrit les yeux.
Finally   Cupid   opened   the   eyes

"Oh!" dit le Soleil, "j'ai vu la couleur des yeux de
Oh   said   the   Sun   I have   seen   the   color   of the   eyes   of

l'Amour. L'Amour a les yeux bleus!" "Mais oui!"
Cupid   Cupid   has   the   eyes   blue   But   yes
                                                (Indeed)

chantèrent les petits oiseaux de la forêt:
sang   the   little   birds   of   the   forest

"L'Amour   a   les   yeux   bleus!"
Cupid   has the   eyes   blue

"Oui,   certainement,"   dit   la   Rose,   "L'Amour   a   les   yeux
Yes   certainly   said the Rose   Cupid   has the eyes

bleus!"
blue

L'Amour   regarda   le   Soleil,   et   dit: "Oh   Soleil,   pourquoi
Cupid   looked at the Sun   and said Oh   Sun   why

êtes-vous   entré   dans   la   forêt?"
are you   entered into   the forest
(have you)

"Oh!"   dit   le   Soleil,   "j'ai   entendu   les   oiseaux   qui
Oh   said the Sun   I have heard   the   birds   who

chantaient: 'Oh,   le   joli   petit   Amour';   et   je   suis   entré
sang   Oh   the pretty little Cupid   and I   am entered
                                                               (have entered)

dans   la   forêt   pour   vous   voir."
into   the forest for   you   to see

L'Amour   dit   au   Soleil,   "Oh   Soleil,   vous   êtes   curieux,
Cupid   said to the Sun   Oh   Sun   you   are   curious

très   curieux."
very   curious

"Oui,"   dit   le   Soleil,   "je   suis   curieux,   mais   la   Rose
Yes   said the Sun   I   am   curious   but   the Rose

vous   a   protégé."
you   has protected

"Merci!   chère   Rose,"   dit   le   joli   petit   Amour,   "merci,
Thanks   dear   Rose   said the pretty little Cupid   thank you
(Thank you)

merci.   Vous   êtes   bien   bonne,   chère   Rose,   et   vous
thank you You   are   well   good   dear   Rose   and you
                         (very)

êtes   aussi   belle   que   bonne.   Quelle   récompense
are   as   beautiful   as   good   What   reward

voulez-vous,   chère   Rose,   vous   qui   êtes   la   plus   belle
want you   dear   Rose   you   who   are   the most   beautiful

de   toutes   les   fleurs?"
of   all   the   flowers

"Oh!"   dit   la   Rose.   "Donnez-moi   un   charme   de   plus!"
Oh   said the Rose   Give me   one   charm   of   more
                                                        ()

"Comment!"   dit   l'Amour,   surpris.
How   said Cupid   surprised

"Vous   demandez   un   charme   de   plus.   Impossible!   Je
You   ask   one   charm   of   more   Impossible   I
                                                                          ()

vous   ai   déjà   donné   tous   les   charmes.   Je   vous   ai
you   have already given   all   the   charms   I   you   have

donné   une   forme   parfaite.   Je   vous   ai   donné   une
given   a   form   perfect   I   you   have given   a

couleur   charmante.   Je   vous   ai   donné   un   parfum
color   charming   I   you   have given   a   perfume

délicat.   Je   vous   ai   donné   tous   les   charmes   et   toutes
delicate   I   you   have given   all   the   charms   and   all

les   grâces,   et   vous   demandez   une   charme   de   plus.
the   graces   and   you   ask   one   charm   of   more
                                                                        ()

Ce   n'est   pas   raisonnable!"
This   not is   not   reasonable
                 ()

"Oh!"   dit   la   Rose,   "raisonnable   ou   pas   raisonnable,   je
Oh   said   the   Rose   reasonable   or   not   reasonable   I

vous   demande   un   attrait   de   plus,   cher   Amour.   Je
you   ask   one   attraction of   more   dear   Cupid   I
                                                    ()

vous   ai   protégé.   Récompensez-moi!"
you   have protected   Reward me

L'Amour dit: "C'est impossible!" Mais la Rose insista.
Cupid said It is impossible But the Rose insisted

Enfin l'Amour, en colère, dit: "Rose, vous êtes belle,
Finally Cupid in anger said Rose you are beautiful

vous êtes la plus belle des fleurs, mais vous n'êtes
you are the most beautiful of the flowers but you not are
(are)

pas bonne." Et l'Amour prit de la mousse. Il jeta la
not good And Love took of the moss He threw the
() ()

mousse sur la Rose, et dit: "Vous ne méritez rien
moss on the Rose and said You not deserve nothing
(no more)

que cela!"
than that

La Rose, couverte de mousse verte, parut plus belle
The Rose covered by moss green appeared more beautiful

que jamais, et la Rose dit avec joie: "Merci, mon joli
than ever and the Rose said with joy Thank you my pretty

petit Amour! Merci, vous m'avez donné une récompense."
little Cupid Thank you you have me given a reward

51　La Rose Mousseuse

"Vous m'avez donné une grâce de plus." "Oui!" dit
You have me given one grace of more Yes said
()

l'Amour, surpris. "Je vous ai donné une grâce de
Cupid surprised I you have given one grace of
()

plus!"
more

Le Soleil regarda la Rose, et dit aussi: "Mais oui! la
The Sun looked at the Rose and said also But yes the

Rose a une grâce de plus." Et tous les petits
Rose has one grace of more And all the little
()

oiseaux chantèrent: "Mais oui, le joli petit Amour a
birds sang But yes the pretty little Cupid has
(Indeed)

donné une grâce de plus à la Rose, à la plus
given one grace of more to the Rose to the most
()

belle des fleurs."
beautiful of the flowers

Et l'Amour partit en chantant aussi: "La Rose
And Cupid left while singing also The Rose

mousseuse est la plus belle des fleurs. Elle est
mossy is the most beautiful of the flowers She is

bonne aussi."
good also

"Elle m'a protégé quand le Soleil est arrivé pour voir
She me has protected when the Sun is arrived for to see
(has) ()

la couleur de mes yeux qui sont bleus."
the color of my eyes who are blue

Et depuis ce jour la Rose, cette coquette, a toujours
And from this day the Rose that flirt has always

porté un peu de mousse verte.
carried a bit of moss green

53   La Rose Mousseuse

LE   CHAT   ET   LE   RENARD
THE   CAT   AND   THE   FOX

Un   paysan   avait   un   chat   qui   était   très   méchant   et   si
A   peasant   had   a   cat   who   was   very   mean   and so

désagréable   que   tout   le   monde   le   détestait.   Le   paysan
unpleasant   that   the whole world   him   hated   The   peasant
                     (everyone)

était   fatigué   de   ce   chat,   et   un   jour   il   le   mit   dans
was   tired   of   this cat   and one day   he   it   put   in

un   grand   sac.   Le   paysan   porta   le   sac   dans   la   forêt,
a   large   bag   The   peasant   carried   the   bag   in   the   forest
                                                          (into)

et   quand   il   fut   arrivé   à   une   grande   distance   de   la
and when   he   was   arrivé   at   a   large   distance   of   the
                  (had)

maison,   il   ouvrit   le   sac,   et   le   méchant   chat   sortit.
house   he   opened   the   bag   and the   malicious   cat   got out

Le   chat   resta   dans   la   forêt,   où   il   trouva   une   petite
The   cat   stayed   in   the   forest   where it   found   a   small

cabane.
hut

Le   chat   demeura   dans   cette   cabane   et   mangea
The   cat   remained   in   this   hut   and   ate

beaucoup   de   souris   et   d'oiseaux.   Un   jour   le   chat   alla
many   of   mice   and   of birds   One   day   the   cat   went
            ()   (birds)

se   promener   dans   la   forêt   et   rencontra   Mademoiselle
to walk around   in   the   forest   and   met   Miss

Renard.   Elle   regarda   le   chat   avec   curiosité,   et   dit:
Fox   She   looked at   the   cat   with   curiosity   and   said

"Mon   beau   monsieur,   qui   êtes-vous?   Que   faites-vous
My   beautiful   mylord   who   are you   What   do you
                     (sir)

dans   la   forêt?"
in   the   forest

"Je   suis   le   bailli   de   la   forêt.   Mon   nom   est   Ivan.
I   am   the   bailiff   of   the   forest   My   name   is   Ivan

J'arrive   de   la   Sibérie   pour   gouverner   cette   forêt."
I come   from   the   Siberia   to   govern   this   forest
                    ()

"Oh,"   dit   Mademoiselle   Renard.   "Je   vous   prie,   Monsieur
Oh   said   Miss   Fox   I   you   request   Sir

le   bailli   de   la   forêt,   venez   dîner   avec   moi."
the   bailiff   of   the   forest   come   to dine   with   me
()

Le chat accepta l'invitation, et au dîner Mademoiselle
The cat accepted the invitation and at the dinner Miss

Renard dit: "Monsieur le bailli, êtes-vous garçon ou
Fox said Sir the bailiff are you boy or
() (single)

marié?"
married

"Je suis garçon," répondit le chat.
I am single answered the cat

"Et moi, je suis demoiselle. Monsieur le bailli,
And me I am miss Sir the baillif
(unmarried woman) (baillif)

épousez-moi!"
marry me

Le chat consentit à ce mariage, qui fut célébré avec
The cat agreed with this marriage which was celebrated with

beaucoup de cérémonie.
much of ceremony
()

Le lendemain du mariage, le chat dit à sa femme:
The following day of the marriage the cat said to his wife

"Madame   Renard,   j'ai   faim;   allez   à   la   chasse   et
Madam   Fox   I have   hunger   go   to   the   hunt   and
                       (am)   (hungry)   ()

apportez-moi   un   bon   dîner."
bring me   a   good   dinner

Madame   Renard   partit.
Madam   Fox   left

Elle   rencontra   le   loup,   qui   dit: "Oh   ma   chère   amie,
She   met   the   wolf   who   said   Oh   my   dear   friend

je   vous   cherche   depuis   longtemps   en   vain.   Où
I   you   seek   since   a long time   in vain   Where

avez-vous   été?"
have you   been

"Chez   mon   mari,   le   bailli   de   la   forêt,   car   je   suis
With   my   husband   the   bailiff   of   the   forest   because I   am

mariée!"
married

"Vous,   mariée!"   dit   le   loup   avec   surprise.   "J'aimerais
You   married   said   the   wolf   with   surprise   I would like

faire   visite   à   votre   mari."
to make   visit   to   your   husband
          (a visit)

"Très-bien," dit Madame Renard, "mais comme mon mari
Very well said Madam Fox but as my husband

est terrible, je vous conseille d'apporter un agneau.
is terrible I you advise of to bring a lamb
(to bring)

Déposez l'agneau à la porte, et cachez-vous; sans cela
Deposit the lamb at the door and hide yourself without that

il vous dévorera."
he you will devour

Le loup courut chercher un agneau pour le chat.
The wolf ran to search for a lamb for the cat

Madame Renard continua sa route. Elle rencontra l'ours.
Madam Fox continued her way She met the bear

L'ours dit: "Bonjour, ma chère amie. D'où venez-vous?"
The bear said Hello my dear friend From where come you
(From where did you come)

"De la maison de mon mari," répondit Madame
From the house of my husband answered Madam

Renard. "Mon mari est le bailli Ivan."
Fox My husband is the bailiff Ivan

"Oh!" dit l'ours, "permettez-moi de faire visite à votre
Oh said the bear allow me to make visit (a visit) to your

mari."
husband

"Certainement," répondit Madame Renard, "mais mon mari
Certainly answered Madam Fox but my husband

a la mauvaise habitude de dévorer tous les animaux
has the bad practice to devour all the animals

qu'il n'aime pas. Allez chercher un boeuf. Apportez-le-lui
that he does not like Go seek an ox Bring it him

en hommage. Le loup apportera un agneau." L'ours
in homage The wolf will bring a lamb The bear

partit; il alla chercher un boeuf. Il rencontra le loup
left he went to seek an ox He met the wolf

avec un agneau. Le loup dit: "Mon ami l'ours, où
with a lamb The wolf said My friend the bear where

allez-vous?"
go you
(are you going)

"Chez le mari de Madame Renard. Je lui porte un
To the husband of Madam Fox I him carry an

boeuf. Où allez-vous, mon cher loup?"
ox Where go you my dear wolf
(are you going)

"Je   vais   aussi   chez   le   mari   de   Madame   Renard.   Je
I   go   also   to   the   husband of   Madam   Fox   I

lui   porte   un   agneau.   Madame   Renard   dit   que   son
him   carry   a   lamb   Madam   Fox   said   that   her

mari   est   terrible!"
husband is   terrible

Les   deux   animaux   continuèrent   leur   route;   ils   arrivèrent
The   two   animals   continued   their   road   they   arrived

bientôt   près   de   la   maison   du   chat.   Le   loup   dit   à
soon   near   by   the   house   of the cat   The   wolf   said   to

l'ours: "Allez,   mon   ami,   frappez   à   la   porte,   et   dites
the bear   Go   my   friend knock   on   the   door   and   say

au   mari   de   Madame   Renard   que   nous   avons   apporté
to the husband of   Madam   Fox   that   we   have   brought

un   boeuf   et   un   agneau."
an   ox   and   a   lamb

"Oh   non!"   dit   l'ours,   "j'ai   peur.   Allez   vous-même!"
Oh   no   said   the bear   I have   fear   Go   yourself
                                  (I am)   (afraid)

"Impossible," dit le loup, "mais voilà le lièvre, il ira
Impossible said the wolf but see there the hare he will go
(there is)

pour nous."
for us

Le lièvre alla à la cabane. Le loup se cacha sous
The hare went to the hut The wolf hid himself under

les feuilles sèches, et l'ours grimpa sur un arbre.
the leaves dry and the bear climbed in a tree

Quelques minutes après Madame Renard arriva avec le
Some minutes later Madam Fox arrived with the

chat, son mari. "Oh!" dit le loup à l'ours. "Le mari
cat her husband Oh said the wolf to the bear The husband

de Madame Renard est très petit."
of Madam Fox is very small

"Oui!" dit l'ours avec mépris, "il est en effet fort
Yes said the bear with contempt he is in effect very

petit!"
small

63 Le Chat Et Le Renard

Le chat arriva. Il sauta sur le boeuf, et dit avec
The cat arrived He jumped on the ox and said with

colère: "C'est peu, très peu!" "Oh!" dit l'ours avec
anger It is little very little Oh said the bear with

surprise; "il est si petit, et il a un si grand appétit!
surprise he is so small and he has a such large appetite

Un taureau est assez grand pour quatre ours. Il est
A bull is enough large for four bears He is

terrible en effet!"
terrible in fact

Le loup, caché sous les feuilles, trembla. Le chat
The wolf hidden under the leaves trembled The cat

entendit un petit bruit dans les feuilles. Il pensa
heard a small noise in the leaves He thought

qu'une souris était cachée sous les feuilles, et il
that a mouse was hidden under the leaves and he

courut et enfonça ses griffes dans le museau du
ran and inserted his claws in the muzzle of the

loup. Le loup pensa que le chat voulait le dévorer,
wolf The wolf thought that the cat wanted him to devour

et il partit vite, vite.
and he left quickly quickly

Le   chat,   qui   avait   peur   du   loup,   sauta   sur   l'arbre.
The   cat   who   had   fear   of the   wolf   jumped   on   the tree
              (was)   (afraid)   (in)

"Oh!"   dit   l'ours.   "Le   chat   m'a   vu,   il   m'a   vu,   il   va
Oh   said   the bear   The   cat   me has   seen   he   me has   seen   he   goes

me   dévorer!"   Et   l'ours   descendit   rapidement   de   l'arbre
me   to devour   And   the bear   went down   quickly   of   the tree

et   suivit   le   loup.
and   followed   the   wolf

Madame   Renard,   qui   avait   tout   vu,   cria: "Mon   mari
Madam   Fox   who   had   all   seen   shouted   My   husband

vous   dévorera,   mon   mari   vous   dévorera!"
you   will devour   my   husband   you   will devour

L'ours   et   le   loup   racontèrent   leurs   aventures   à   tous
The bear   and   the   wolf   told   their   adventures   to   all

les   autres   animaux   de   la   forêt,   et   tous   les   animaux
the   other   animals   of   the   forest   and   all   the   animals

avaient   peur   du   chat.
had   fear   of the   cat
(were)   (afraid)

Mais   le   chat   et   Madame   Renard   étaient   très   heureux,
But   the   cat   and   Madam   Fox   were   very   happy

car   ils   avaient   beaucoup   de   viande   à   manger.
because they had   much   of   meat   to   eat
                                     ()

LA VILLE SUBMERGÉE
THE CITY SUBMERGED

Il y avait une fois, en Hollande, une grande et belle
It there had   one   time   in   Holland   a   large   and   beautiful
(There was)

ville appelée Stavoren. Cette ville était située près de
city   called   Stavoren   This   city   was   located   near   of

la mer, et les habitants étaient très riches, parce que
the   sea   and   the   inhabitants   were   very   rich   because

leurs vaisseaux allaient dans toutes les différentes
their   vessels   went   in   all   the   different

parties du monde chercher les trésors de toutes les
parts   of the   world   to seek   the   treasures   of   all   the

différentes contrées. Les habitants de Stavoren étaient
different   regions   The   inhabitants   of   Stavoren   were

très riches, et ils étaient fiers de leur or, fiers de
very   rich   and   they   were   proud   of   their   gold   proud   of

leur argent, fiers de leurs vaisseaux, et fiers de leurs
their   silver   proud   of   their   vessels   and   proud   of   their
                                                            (ships)

grands palais.
large   palaces

Ils   étaient   fiers   et   égoïstes   aussi,   parce   qu'ils   ne
They   were   proud   and   egoists   also   because they   not

pensaient   jamais   aux   pauvres,   qui   n'avaient   ni   or,   ni
thought   ever   of the poor   who   did not have neither gold nor

argent,   ni   vaisseaux,   ni   palais.
silver   nor   ships   nor   palaces

Il   y   avait   une   dame   à   Stavoren   qui   était   plus   riche
It there had   a   lady   in   Stavoren   who   was   more   rich
(There was)

et   plus   fière   que   tous   les   autres   habitants;   elle   était
and   more   proud   than   all   the   other   inhabitants; she   was

aussi   plus   égoïste   et   plus   cruelle   envers   les   pauvres.
also   more   egoist   and   more   cruel   towards   the   poor

Un   jour,   cette   dame   si   riche   appela   le   capitaine   de
One   day   this   lady   so   rich   called   the   captain   of

son   plus   grand   vaisseau,   et   dit:
her   most   large   vessel   and   said

"Capitaine,   préparez   votre   vaisseau,   et   quittez   le   port."
Captain   prepare   your   vessel   and   leave   the   port
                                    (ship)

"Allez   me   chercher   une   grande   cargaison   de   la   chose
Go   me   search   a   large   cargo   of   the   thing
(for me)

la   plus   précieuse   du   monde."
the   most   precious   of the   world

"Certainement,   madame,"   dit   le   capitaine,   "commandez,   et
Certainly   my lady   said   the   captain   order   and

j'obéirai.   Mais   que   voulez-vous,   madame?   Voulez-vous
I will obey   But   what   want you   Madam   Want you
(do you want)   (Do you want)

une   grande   cargaison   d'or,   d'argent,   de   pierres
a   large   cargo   of gold   of silver   of   stones

précieuses,   ou   d'étoffes?   Que   voulez-vous?"
precious   or   of fabrics   What   want you
(do you want)

"Capitaine,"   répondit   la   dame,   "j'ai   donné   mes   ordres.
Captain   answered   the   lady   I have   given   my   orders

Je   demande   une   cargaison   de   la   chose   la   plus
I   ask   a   cargo   of   the   thing   the   most

précieuse   du   monde."
precious   of the   world
(in the)

"Il y a seulement une chose qui est plus précieuse
It there has only one thing that is more precious
(There is)

que toutes les autres. Allez chercher cette chose-là et
than all the others Go seek that thing there and
(thing)

partez immédiatement."
leave immediately

Le pauvre capitaine, qui avait peur de la dame, lui
The poor captain who had fear of the lady her
(was) (afraid)

obéit. Il alla au port, il prépara son vaisseau, et
obeyed He went to the port he prepared his vessel and
(ship)

partit. Alors il appela ses officiers et ses matelots, et
left Then he called his officers and his sailors and

dit:
said

"Camarades, notre maîtresse a commandé une grande
Comrades our mistress has ordered a large

cargaison de la chose la plus précieuse du monde.
cargo of the thing the most precious of the world

Elle a refusé de dire quelle est la chose la plus
She has refused to say what is the thing the most

précieuse du monde."
precious of the world

"Je ne sais pas quelle est la chose la plus précieuse
I not know (do not know) which is the thing the most precious

du monde. Savez-vous quelle est la chose la plus
of the world Know you which is the thing the most

précieuse du monde?"
inprecious of the world

"Oui, mon capitaine," répondit un officier, "la chose la
Yes my captain answered an officer the thing the

plus précieuse du monde, c'est l'or."
most precious of the world that is the gold (gold)

"Oh, non, mon capitaine," répondit un autre officier, "la
Oh no my captain answered an other officer the

chose la plus précieuse du monde, c'est l'argent."
thing the most precious of the world it is the silver

"Non," dit un autre. "Mes camarades, la chose la plus
No said another My comrades the thing the most

précieuse du monde ce sont les pierres précieuses, les
precious of the world this are the stones precious (gems) the

perles, les diamants, et les rubis."
pearls the diamonds and the ruby

Un autre matelot dit: "Mon capitaine, la chose la plus
Another sailor said My captain the thing the most

précieuse du monde ce sont les étoffes."
precious of the world this are the fabrics

Tous les hommes et tous les officiers avaient une
All the men and all the officers had an

opinion différente, et le pauvre capitaine était très
opinion different and the poor captain was very

embarrassé.
embarrassed

Enfin le capitaine dit: "Je sais quelle est la chose la
Finally the captain said I know what is the thing the

plus précieuse du monde, c'est le blé. Avec le blé
most precious of the world it is the grain With the grain

on fait le pain, la chose la plus précieuse du
one makes the bread the thing the most precious of the

monde, parce que le pain est indispensable." Le capitaine
world the bread is indispensable The captain

était content, et tous les hommes étaient contents aussi.
was satisfied and all the men were satisfied also

Le capitaine dirigea son vaisseau dans la mer Baltique.
The captain directed his vessel in the sea Baltic
(steered) (ship)

Il alla à la ville de Dantzic. Là il acheta une
He went to the city of Danzig There he bought a

grande cargaison de blé magnifique. Il chargea la
large cargo of grain splendid He loaded the

cargaison de blé sur son vaisseau, et il repartit pour
cargo of grain on his vessel and he left again for

Stavoren. Pendant son absence, la dame avait fait
Stavoren During his absence the lady had made

visite à toutes les personnes riches de Stavoren, et
visit to all the people rich of Stavoren and
(a visit)

avait dit: "J'ai envoyé mon capitaine chercher une
had said I have send my captain to seek a

cargaison de la chose la plus précieuse du monde."
cargo of the thing the most precious of the world

"Ah," répondaient les personnes riches, "quelle est cette
Ah answered the people rich what is this

chose?"
thing

Mais la dame refusait de répondre et disait seulement:
But the lady refused to answer and said only

"Devinez, mes amis, devinez."
Guess my friends guess

Naturellement la curiosité de toutes les personnes de
Naturally the curiosity of all the people of

Stavoren était grande, et elles attendaient le retour du
Stavoren was great and they awaited the return of the

capitaine avec impatience. Un jour le grand vaisseau
captain with impatience One day the large vessel (ship)

arriva dans le port, le capitaine se présenta devant la
arrived in the port the captain himself presented before the

dame qui le regarda avec surprise, et dit:
lady who him looked at with surprise and said

"Comment, capitaine, déjà de retour! Vous avez été
How captain already of return You have been
(Why)

rapide comme un pigeon."
fast as a pigeon

"Avez-vous   la   cargaison   que   j'ai   demandée?"
Have you   the   cargo   that   I have asked

"Oui,   madame,"   répondit   le   capitaine,   "j'ai   une   cargaison
Yes   Madam   answered   the   captain   I have a   cargo

du   plus   magnifique   blé!"
of the most   splendid   grain

"Comment!"   dit   la   dame.   "Une   cargaison   de   blé!
How   said   the   lady   A   cargo   of   grain
(How do you mean)
Misérable!   j'ai   demandé   une   cargaison   de   la   chose   la
Miserable wretch   I have   asked   a   cargo   of   the   thing   the

plus   précieuse   du   monde,   et   vous   apportez   une   chose
most   precious   of the   world   and   you   bring   a   thing

aussi   vulgaire,   aussi   ordinaire,   aussi   commune   que   du
as   vulgar   as   ordinary   as   common   as   of the
                                                                                                      ()
blé!"
grain

"Pardon,   madame,"   dit   le   capitaine.
Forgive   madam   said   the   captain
(Forgive me)

"Le blé n'est pas vulgaire, ordinaire, et commun. Le
The grain is not vulgar ordinary and common The

blé est très précieux. C'est la chose la plus précieuse
grain is very precious It is the thing the most precious

du monde. Avec le blé on fait le pain. Et le pain,
of the world With the grain one makes the bread And the bread

madame, est indispensable."
madam is indispensable

"Misérable!" dit la dame. "Allez au port, immédiatement,
Miserable wretch said the lady Go to the port immediately

et jetez toute la cargaison de blé à la mer."
and throw all the cargo of grain into the sea

"Oh, madame, quel dommage!" dit le capitaine. "Le blé
Oh my lady what waste said the captain The grain
(a waste)

est si bon! Si vous ne voulez pas ce bon blé,
is so good If you not want this good grain

donnez-le aux pauvres, ils ont faim, ils seront contents."
give it to the poor they have hunger they will be satisfied
(are) (hungry)

Mais la dame refusa, et dit encore une fois:
But the lady refused and said again one time

"Capitaine, allez au port, immédiatement, et jetez toute
Captain go to the port immediately and throw whole

la cargaison de blé à la mer! J'arriverai au port
the cargo of grain into the sea I will arrive in the port

dans quelques minutes pour voir exécuter mes ordres."
in some minutes to watch to carry out my orders
                                  (carrying out)

Le pauvre capitaine partit.
The poor captain left

En route il rencontra beaucoup de pauvres, et dit:
On way he met many of poor people and said
  (the way)   ()

"Ma maîtresse, la dame la plus riche de Stavoren, a
My mistress the lady the most rich of Stavoren has

une grande cargaison de blé. Elle ne veut pas ce
a large cargo of grain She wants not this
                                    (does not want)

blé."
grain

"Elle a commandé de jeter toute la cargaison à la
She has ordered to throw all the cargo into the

mer. Si vous voulez le blé, venez au port, peut-être
sea If you want the grain come to the port maybe

que ma maîtresse aura compassion de vous, et vous
that my mistress will have compassion of you and you
(with)

donnera toute la cargaison."
will give all the cargo

Cinq minutes plus tard tous les pauvres de Stavoren
Five minutes more late all the the poor of Stavoren
(later)

étaient assemblés sur le quai; la dame arriva, et dit:
were assembled on the quay the lady arrived and said

"Capitaine, avez-vous exécuté mes ordres?"
Captain have you carried out my orders

"Non, madame, pas encore!"
No Madam not yet

"Alors, capitaine, obéissez, jetez toute la cargaison de
Then captain obey throw all the cargo of

blé à la mer."
grain into the sea

"Madame," dit le capitaine, "regardez tous ces pauvres,
Madam said the captain look at all these poor people

ils ont faim! Donnez le blé que vous ne voulez pas
they have hunger Give the grain that you want not
(are) (hungry)

aux pauvres!"
to the the poor

"Oh, oui, madame! Nous avons faim, nous avons faim,"
Oh yes madam We have hunger we have hunger
(are) (hungry) (are) (hungry)

crièrent les pauvres. "Donnez-nous le blé! Donnez-nous
shouted the poor Give us the grain Give us

le blé!"
the grain

Mais la dame était très cruelle, et dit:
But the lady was very cruel and said

"Non,   non!   Capitaine,   j'ai   commandé.   Jetez   tout   le   blé
No   no   Captain   I have ordered   Throw   all   the grain

à   la   mer,   immédiatement."
into the   sea   immediately

"Jamais,   madame!"   répondit   le   capitaine.   Alors   la   dame
Never   madam   answered   the captain   Then   the lady

fit   un   signe   aux   officiers   et   aux   matelots,   et   répéta
made a   sign   to the officers   and to the sailors   and repeated

son   ordre.   Les   hommes   obéirent,   et   malgré   les   cris
her   order   The   men   obeyed   and in spite of the cries

des   pauvres,   et   malgré   leurs   pleurs,   tout   le   blé   fut
of the poor   and in spite of their   tears   all   the grain was

jeté   à   la   mer.
thrown into the   sea

La   dame   regarda   en   silence,   et   quand   la   procession
The lady   watched   in   silence   and when   the procession

de   sacs   eut   cessé,   elle   demanda   aux   officiers   et   aux
of   bags   had   ceased   she   asked   of the officers   and of the

matelots:
sailors

"Avez-vous jeté tout le blé à la mer?"
Have you   thrown all the grain into the sea

"Oui, madame," répondirent les hommes.
Yes   madam   answered   the men

"Oui, madame," dit le capitaine d'une voix indignée,
Yes   madam   said the captain   with a voice indignant

"mais un   jour arrivera   où   vous regretterez ce   que
but   a   day   will arrive where you   will regret   this what
       (one)   (when)

vous avez fait! Un   jour arrivera   où   vous aurez   faim!
you   have done   A   day   will arrive where you   will have hunger
                   (One)   (when)   (be)   (hungry)

Un   jour arrivera   où   personne n'aura compassion de
One   day   will arrive where nobody will have compassion of
                                                              (with)

vous!"
you

La   dame regarda   le   capitaine avec surprise, et   dit:
The lady looked at the captain   with surprise   and said

"Capitaine, c'est   impossible."
Captain   that is impossible

"Je suis la personne la plus riche de Stavoren. Moi,
I am the person the most rich of Stavoren Me
(richest)

avoir faim, c'est absurde!"
to have hunger it is absurd
(to be hungry)

Alors la dame prit une bague de diamants, la jeta à
Then the lady took a ring of diamonds it threw into

la mer, et dit: "Capitaine, quand cette bague de
the sea and said Captain when this ring of

diamants sera placée dans ma main, je croirai ce que
diamonds will be placed in my hand I will believe that what

vous avez dit!" et la dame quitta le port.
you have said and the lady left the port

Quelques jours après, un domestique trouva la bague
Some days afterwards a servant found the ring

de diamants dans l'estomac d'un poisson qu'il préparait
of diamonds in the stomach of a fish that he prepared

pour le dîner de la dame.
for the dinner of the lady

Il porta la bague à sa maîtresse. Elle regarda la
He carried the ring to his mistress She looked at the

bague avec surprise, et demanda: "Où avez-vous trouvé
ring with surprise and asked Where have you found

cette bague?" Le domestique répondit: "Madame, j'ai
this ring The servant answered Madam I have

trouvé la bague dans l'estomac d'un poisson!"
found the ring in the stomach of a fish

Alors la dame pensa aux paroles du capitaine. Le
Then the lady thought at the words of the captain The

même jour la dame reçut la nouvelle de la
same day the lady received the news of the

destruction de tous ses vaisseaux, et elle perdit aussi
destruction of all her vessels and she lost also

tout son or, tout son argent, toutes ses
all her gold all her silver all her

pierres précieuses, et tous ses palais.
gems and all her palaces

La	dame	n'était	plus	riche,	mais	elle	était	pauvre,	très
The	lady	was not anymore		rich	but	she	was	poor	very

pauvre.	Elle	alla	de	porte	en	porte,	demander
poor	She	went	from	door	to	door	to ask

quelque	chose	à	manger,	mais	tous	les	riches	et	tous
something		to	eat	but	all	the	rich	and	all

les	pauvres	de	Stavoren	refusèrent	de	lui	donner	du
the	poor	of	Stavoren	refused	of (to)	her	give	of the ()

pain.	La	pauvre	dame	périt	enfin	de	froid	et	de	faim.
bread	The	poor	lady	perished	finally	of	cold	and	of	hunger

Les	autres	personnes	riches	de	Stavoren
The	other	people	rich	of	Stavoren

ne	changèrent	pas	leurs	habitudes.	Alors	le	bon	Dieu,
	changed not		their	practices	Then	the	good	God

qui	n'aime	pas	les	personnes	égoïstes,	envoya	un
who	does not like		the ()	persons (people)	egoistic	sent	a

second	avertissement.
second	warning

Un   jour,   le   port   de   Stavoren   se   trouva   bloqué   par
One day   the port of   Stavoren   itself found   blocked by

un   grand   banc   de   sable.   Ce   banc   empêcha   le
a   large   sandbank   This bank   prevented the

commerce,   et   dans   quelques   jours   le   blé   que   la
trade   and in   some   days   the grain that the

dame   avait   jeté   à   la   mer,   commença   à   pousser,   et
lady   had   thrown into the sea   started   to grow   and

le   banc   de   sable   était   tout   couvert   d'herbe   verte.
the sandbank   was   totally covered with plants green

Toutes   les   personnes   de   Stavoren   regardèrent   le   blé   et
All   the   people   of   Stavoren   looked at   the grain and

dirent: "C'est   un   miracle,   c'est   un   miracle!"   Mais,   le
said   It is   a   miracle   it is   a   miracle   But   the

blé   ne   produisit   pas   de   fruit!   Le   commerce   avait   cessé;
grain produced no   of   fruit   The trade   had   ceased
                                  ()

les   riches   avaient   assez   à   manger,   mais   les   pauvres
the   rich   had   enough to eat   but   the   poor

étaient   plus   pauvres   qu'avant.
were   more   poor   than before

Alors Dieu envoya un troisième avertissement. Un jour,
Then God sent a third warning One day

un homme arriva dans la maison où tous les riches
a man arrived in the house where all the rich people

étaient assemblés, et dit; "J'ai trouvé onze poissons
were assembled and said I have found eleven fish

dans le puits! La digue est rompue. La digue est
in the well The dike is broken The dike is

rompue. Protégez la ville, protégez les maisons des
broken Protect the city protect the houses the

pauvres près de la digue!"
poor near of the dam
()

Mais les riches continuèrent à danser. La mer entra
But the rich people continued to dance The sea entered

dans la ville pendant la nuit, et tout à coup toutes
in the city during the night and all at strike all
(in one strike)

les maisons et tous les palais de Stavoren furent
the houses and all the palaces of Stavoren were

submergés.
submerged

Les   pauvres   périrent,   les   riches   périrent   aussi,   et   le
The   poor   perished   the   rich   perished   also   and   the

Zuidersée   occupe   maintenant   la   place   de   la   belle   ville
Zuiderzee   occupies   now   the   place   of   the   beautiful city
(Southsea which is now a lake called IJsselmeer in the Netherlands)

de   Stavoren,   détruite   à cause   de   l'égoïsme   de   ses
of   Stavoren   destroyed   because   of   the selfishness of   its

habitants   riches   qui   refusaient   de   donner   à   manger   aux
citizens   rich   who   refused   to   give   to   eat   to the

pauvres.
poor

91 La Ville Submergee

LES   QUATRE   SAISONS
THE   FOUR   SEASONS

Il y avait une fois une petite fille. Cette petite fille
It there had one time a little girl This little girl
(There was)

demeurait dans une jolie petite maison avec sa mère
resided in a pretty little house with her mother
(lived)

et sa soeur.
and her sister

La petite fille, Laura, était bonne et très jolie. La
The little girl Laura was good and very pretty The

soeur de la petite fille, Claire, était méchante et laide.
sister of the little girl Claire was malicious and ugly

La mère était aussi méchante et laide. La mère
The mother was also malicious and ugly The mother

aimait Claire, mais elle n'aimait pas Laura.
liked Claire but she did not like Laura

Un jour la méchante fille dit à sa mère: "Ma mère,
One day the malicious girl said to her mother My mother

envoyez Laura à la forêt cueillir sept violettes.
send Laura to the forest to pick seven violets

La   mère   répondit: "Des   violettes,   dans   cette   saison!
The mother answered   Of the violets   in   this   season
                                  ()

C'est   impossible,   ma   fille,   dans   la   forêt   il y a
That is impossible   my   daughter   in   the   forest   it there has
                                                             (there is)

seulement   de   la   neige   et   de   la   glace."
only   of   the   snow   and   of   the   ice
             ()   ()   ()   ()

Mais   la   méchante   fille   insista,   et   la   mère   dit   à
But   the   mean   girl   insisted   and   the   mother   said   to

Laura: "Allez   à   la   forêt   cueillir   un   bouquet   de   sept
Laura   Go   to   the   forest   to pick   a   bouquet   of   seven

violettes   pour   votre   soeur."
violets   for   your   sister

Laura   regarda   sa   mère   avec   surprise,   et   répondit: "Ma
Laura   looked at   her   mother   with   surprise   and   answered   My

mère,   c'est   impossible!   Dans   cette   saison   il y a
mother   that is   impossible   In   this   season   it there has
                                                         (there is)

seulement   de   la   neige   et   de   la   glace   dans   la   forêt."
only   of   the   snow   and   of   the   ice   in   the   forest
             ()   ()   ()   ()

Mais   la   mère   insista,   et   la   pauvre   Laura   partit.
But   the   mother   insisted   and   the   poor   Laura   left
                                        ()

Elle alla à la forêt, chercha les violettes, et trouva
She went to the forest searched for the violets and found

seulement de la neige et de la glace. La pauvre fille
only of the snow and of the ice The poor girl
() () () ()

dit: "J'ai froid; où y a-t-il du feu?" Elle regarda à
said I have cold where there has it of the fire She looked to
(I am) (is) ()

droite, elle regarda à gauche, et elle vit un grand
right she looked to left and she saw a large
(the right) (the left)

feu à une grande distance. Elle alla à ce feu, et
fire at a great distance She went to this fire and

vit douze hommes assis autour du feu. Trois hommes
saw twelve men sitting around of the fire Three men
(the)

avaient de longues barbes blanches et de longues
had of long beards white and of long
() ()

robes blanches; trois hommes avaient de longues barbes
robes white three men had of long beards
()

blondes et de longues robes vertes; trois hommes
blond and of long robes green three men
()

avaient de longues barbes brunes et de longues robes
had of long beards brown and of long robes
() ()

jaunes, et trois hommes avaient de longues barbes
yellow and three men had of long beards
()

noires et de longues robes violettes.
black and of long robes purple
()

La petite fille s'approcha en silence, et elle vit qu'un
The little girl herself approached in silence and she saw that one
(approached)

des hommes à barbe blanche avait un bâton à la
of the men with (a) beard white had a staff in the

main.
hand

Cet homme se tourna et dit:
This man himself turned and said
(turned around)

"Petite fille, que cherchez vous dans la forêt?"
Little girl what seek you in the forest

La petite fille répondit:
The little girl answered

"Monsieur, je cherche des violettes."
Sir I search of the violets
()

L'homme à barbe blanche dit: "Ma pauvre petite fille,
The man with (a) beard white said My poor little girl

ce n'est pas la saison des violettes, c'est la saison
this is not not the season of the violets it is the season
()

de la neige et de la glace."
of the snow and of the ice

"Oui,"   dit   la   petite   fille,   "mais   ma   mère   a   dit: 'Allez
Yes   said   the   little   girl   but   my   mother   has   said   Go

à   la   forêt   cueillir   un   bouquet   de   violettes   pour   votre
to   the   forest   to pick   a   bouquet   of   violets   for   your

soeur,' et   je   suis   forcée   d'obéir."
sister   and   I   am   forced   of to obey
                                  (to obey)

L'homme   à   barbe   blanche   regarda   la   petite   fille   un
The man   with   (a) beard   white   looked at   the   little   girl   a

instant,   et   dit:
moment   and   said

"Chauffez-vous,   ma   pauvre   enfant."
Warm yourself   my   poor   child

Alors   il   prit   son   bâton,   se   tourna   vers   un   des
Then   he   took   his   staff   turned himself   towards   one   of the
                                (turned)

hommes   à   barbe   blonde,   lui   donna   le   bâton   et   dit:
men   with   (a) beard   blond   him   gave   the   staff   and   said

"Frère   Mai,   les   violettes   sont   votre   affaire.   Voulez-vous
Brother   May   the   violets   are   your   business   Will you

aider   cette   petite   fille?"
help   this   little   girl

"Certainement,"   répondit   Frère   Mai.   Il   prit   le   bâton   et
Certainly   answered   Brother May   He   took   the staff   and

attisa   le   feu.   En   un   instant   la   glace   disparut,   et   la
poked   the fire   In   one moment   the ice   disappeared and the

neige   aussi.   La   petite   fille   n'avait   plus   froid,   elle   avait
snow   also   The little   girl   did not have anymore cold   she   had
                                       (was not)   (felt)

chaud.   Un   instant   après   elle   vit   que   l'herbe   était
warm   One moment   afterwards she saw   that the grass was

verte,   et   bientôt   elle   vit   beaucoup   de   violettes   dans
green   and soon   she   saw   many   of   violets   in
                                                ()

l'herbe.
the grass

Alors   Frère   Mai   se   tourna   vers   elle   et   dit: "Ma   chère
Then   Brother May   turned himself towards her   and said My   dear
                      (turned)

petite   fille,   cueillez   un   bouquet   de   violettes,   aussi   vite
little   girl   pick   a   bouquet   of   violets   as   quickly

que   possible,   et   partez."   La   petite   fille   cueillit   un
as   possible   and leave   The little   girl   picked   a

bouquet   de   sept   violettes,   dit: "Merci,   mon   bon
bouquet   of   seven violets   said   Thank you my   good

monsieur   Mai,"   et   partit.
sir   May   and left

Frère **Mai** donna le bâton à l'homme à barbe
Brother May gave the staff to the man with (a) beard

blanche, il attisa le feu, et en un instant les violettes
white he poked the fire and in one moment the violets

et l'herbe avaient disparu, et la glace et la neige
and the grass had disappeared and the ice and the snow

étaient là comme avant.
were there like before

La petite fille alla à la maison et frappa à la porte.
The little girl went to the house and knocked on the door

La mère ouvrit la porte et dit: "Avez-vous les sept
The mother opened the door and said "Have you the seven

violettes?"
violets

"Oui, ma mère," répondit Laura, et elle donna les
Yes my mother answered Laura and she gave the

violettes à sa mère.
violets to her mother

"Où avez-vous trouvé ces violettes?" dit la mère.
Where have you found these violets said the mother

"Dans la forêt," répondit Laura, "il y avait beaucoup
In the forest answered Laura it there had many
() (were)

de violettes dans l'herbe."
of violets in the grass
()

La mère de Laura était très surprise, mais elle ne
The mother of Laura was very surprised but she not

dit rien.
said nothing

Le lendemain la méchante fille dit à sa mère: "Ma
The following day the malicious girl said to her mother My

mère, envoyez Laura à la forêt cueillir huit fraises."
mother send Laura to the forest to pick eight strawberries

"Des fraises, dans cette saison, c'est impossible, ma
Of the strawberries in this season that is impossible my
() (Strawberries)

fille," répondit la mère.
daughter answered the mother

Mais Claire insista, et la mère dit à Laura: "Allez à
But Claire insisted and the mother said to Laura Go to

la forêt cueillir huit fraises pour votre soeur."
the forest to pick eight strawberries for your sister

Laura	regarda	sa	mère	avec	surprise,	et	dit:	"Ma
Laura	looked at	her	mother	with	surprise	and	said	My

mère,	c'est	impossible!	Dans	cette	saison	il	y	a	de
mother	that is	impossible	In	this	season	it	there	has	of
						()		(is)	()

la	glace	et	de	la	neige	dans	la	forêt	mais	pas	de
the	ice	and	of	the	snow	in	the	forest	but	not	of
()			()	()							()

fraises."
strawberries

Mais	la	mère	insista,	et	la	pauvre	Laura	partit.
But	the	mother	insisted	and	the	poor	Laura	left

Elle	alla	à	la	forêt,	chercha	les	fraises,	et	trouva
She	went	to	the	forest	sought	the	strawberries	and	found

seulement	de	la	neige	et	de	la	glace.	La	pauvre	fille
only	of	the	snow	and	of	the	ice	The	poor	girl
	()	()			()	()				

dit:	"J'ai	froid!	où	y	a-t-il	du	feu?"	Elle	regarda	à
said	I have	cold	where	there has it		of the	fire	She	looked	to
	(I am)			(is there)		()				

droite	et	à	gauche,	et	elle	vit	un	grand	feu	à	une
right	and	to	left	and	she	saw	a	large	fire	at	a
(the right)			(the left)								

grande	distance.	Elle	s'approcha	de	ce	feu	et	vit	les
great	distance	She	herself approached	of	this	fire	and	saw	the
			(approached)	()					

douze	hommes.
twelve	men

Trois — Three
hommes — men
avaient — had
des — of the ()
barbes — beards
blanches — white
et — and
des — of the ()

robes — robes
blanches, — white
trois — three
hommes — men
avaient — had
des — of the ()
barbes — beards

blondes — blond
et — and
des — of the ()
robes — robes
vertes, — green
trois — three
hommes — men
avaient — had
des — of the ()

barbes — beards
brunes — brown
et — and
des — of the ()
robes — robes
jaunes, — yellow
et — and
trois — three
hommes — men

avaient — had
des — of the ()
barbes — beards
noires — black
et — and
des — of the ()
robes — robes
violettes. — purple

La — The
petite — little
fille — girl
s'approcha — herself approached (approached)
et — and
dit — said
à — to
l'homme — the man
à — with
barbe — (a) beard

blanche — white
qui — who
avait — had
un — a
bâton — staff
à — in
la — the
main: — hand
"Monsieur, — Sir
j'ai — I have (I am)

froid, — cold
voulez-vous — will you
me — me
permettre — allow
de — to
me — myself
chauffer — warm
à — at
votre — your

feu?" — fire

"Certainement," — Certainly
répondit — answered
l'homme. — the man
"Mon — My
enfant, — child
que — what

cherchez-vous — seek you (do you search)
dans — in
la — the
forêt — forest
dans — in
cette — this
saison?" — season

"Des   fraises,   monsieur."
Of the strawberries sir
()   (Strawberries)

"Des   fraises,"   répéta   l'homme   avec   surprise,   "ce   n'est
Of the strawberries repeated   the man   with   surprise   this   not is
()   (Strawberries)   (is)

pas   la   saison   des   fraises.   C'est   la   saison   de   la
not   the   season   of the strawberries It is   the   season   of   the

glace   et   de   la   neige."
ice   and   of   the   snow

La   petite   fille   répondit: "Ma   mère   a   dit, 'Allez   à   la
The   little   girl   answered   My   mother   has   said Go   to   the

forêt   cueillir   des   fraises   pour   votre   soeur,' et   je   suis
forest   to pick   of the strawberries for   your   sister   and   I   am
                     ()

forcée   d'obéir."
forced   of to obey
          (to obey)

Alors   l'homme   à   barbe   blanche   donna   son   bâton   à   un
Then   the man   with (a) beard white   gave   his   staff   to   one

des   hommes   à   barbe   brune,   et   dit: "Frère   Juin,   les
of the men   with (a) beard brown   and   said   Brother   June   the

fraises   sont   votre   affaire.   Voulez-vous   aider   cette   petite
strawberries are   your   business   Will you   help   this   little

fille?"
girl

"Avec le plus grand plaisir," répondit Frère Juin. Il prit
With the greatest pleasure answered Brother June He took

le bâton et attisa le feu. En un instant toute la
the staff and poked the fire In one moment all the

neige et toute la glace avaient disparu. La petite fille
snow and all the ice had disappeared The little girl

n'avait plus froid, elle avait chaud. Elle vit l'herbe
did not have more cold she had warm She saw the grass
(felt) (anymore) (felt)

verte, et quelques minutes après elle vit beaucoup de
green and some minutes afterwards she saw many of
()

fraises dans l'herbe.
strawberries in the grass

Alors Frère Juin se tourna vers elle et dit, "Ma chère
Then Brother June himself turned towards her and said My dear
(turned)

petite fille, cueillez vos fraises, vite, vite, et partez."
little girl pick your strawberries quickly quickly and leave

La petite fille cueillit les huit fraises, dit: "Merci, mon
The little girl picked the eight strawberries said Thank you my

bon monsieur Juin," et partit.
good sir June and left

Frère **Juin** donna le bâton à Frère Janvier. Il attisa
Brother June gave the staff to Brother January He poked

le feu et en un instant les fraises avaient disparu, et
the fire and in one moment the strawberries had disappeared and

la neige et la glace étaient là comme avant.
the snow and the ice were there like before

La petite fille retourna à la maison et frappa à la
The little girl turned back to the house and knocked on the

porte. La mère ouvrit la porte, et demanda: "Où sont
door The mother opened the door and asked Where are

les huit fraises?" Laura donna les fraises à sa mère.
the eight strawberries Laura gave the strawberries to her mother

"Où avez-vous trouvé ces fraises?" demanda la mère.
Where have you found these strawberries asked the mother

"Dans la forêt ;" répondit la petite fille, "il y avait
In the forest answered the little girl It there had
(There were)

beaucoup de fraises dans l'herbe." La mère était très
many of strawberries in the grass The mother was very
()

surprise.
surprised

Elle donna les fraises à la méchante fille, qui les
She gave the strawberries to the malicious girl who them

mangea toutes.
ate all

Le lendemain la méchante fille dit à sa mère: "Ma
The following day the malicious girl said to her mother My

mère, envoyez Laura à la forêt cueillir neuf pommes."
mother send Laura to the forest to pick nine apples

La mère dit: "Ma fille, il n'y a pas de pommes dans
The mother said My daughter it not there has not of apples in
(there are no) ()

la forêt dans cette saison." Mais la méchante fille
the forest in this season But the malicious girl

insista, et la mère dit à Laura: "Ma fille, allez dans
insisted and the mother said to Laura My daughter go into

la forêt cueillir neuf pommes pour votre soeur."
the forest to pick nine apples for your sister

Laura regarda sa mère avec surprise et dit: "Mais,
Laura looked at her mother with surprise and said But

ma mère, il n'y a pas de pommes dans la forêt
my mother It not there has not of apples in the forest
() (there) (are) (no) ()

dans cette saison." La mère insista, et Laura partit.
in this season The mother insisted and Laura left

Elle regarda à droite et à gauche, mais elle ne
She looked to right and to left but she not
(the right) (the left) ()

trouva pas de pommes. Elle avait froid, et dit: "Où y
found not of apples She had cold and said Where there
(no) () (was)

a-t-il du feu?"
has it of the fire
(is) ()

Dans un instant elle vit le même feu et les mêmes
In a moment she saw the same fire and the same

hommes.
men

Elle s'approcha et dit à l'homme à barbe blanche qui
She herself approached and said to the man with (a) beard white who
(approached)

avait le bâton à la main: "Mon bon monsieur,
had the staff in the hand My good sir

voulez-vous me permettre de me chauffer à votre feu?"
will you me allow to myself warm at your fire

L'homme répondit: "Certainement, ma pauvre enfant; que
The man answered Certainly my poor child what

cherchez-vous dans la forêt dans cette saison?" "Je
seek you in the forest in this season I
(do you search)

cherche des pommes, monsieur."
search of the apples sir
()

"C'est la saison de la neige et de la glace, ma
It is the season of the snow and of the ice my

pauvre enfant, ce n'est pas la saison des pommes."
poor child this is not not the season of the apples

"Oui, monsieur, mais ma mère a dit: 'Allez chercher
Yes sir but my mother has said Go search

des pommes,' et je suis forcée d'obéir," dit Laura.
of the apples and I am forced of to obey said Laura
()   (to obey)

Alors l'homme à barbe blanche prit son bâton,
Then the man with (a) beard white took its staff

se tourna vers un des hommes à barbe noire et dit:
turned himself towards one of the men with (a) beard black and said
(turned)

"Frère Septembre, les pommes sont votre affaire.
Brother September the apples are your business

Voulez-vous aider cette pauvre petite fille?"
Will you help this poor little girl

"Certainement," répondit Frère Septembre.
Certainly answered Brother September

Il prit le bâton, attisa le feu, et dans un instant la
He took the staff poked the fire and in an moment the

petite fille vit un pommier, tout couvert de pommes.
little girl saw an apple tree totally covered of (with) apples

Alors Frère Septembre se tourna vers la petite fille, et
Then Brother September himself turned (turned) towards the little girl and

dit: "Ma chère petite fille, cueillez votre pommes, vite,
said My dear little girl pick your apples quickly

vite, et partez."
quickly and leave

La petite fille cueillit neuf pommes rouges, dit: "Merci,
The little girl picked nine apples red said Thank you

mon bon monsieur," et partit.
my good sir and left

Frère Septembre donna le bâton à Frère Janvier, qui
Brother September gave the staff to Brother January who

attisa le feu, et à l'instant le pommier disparut, et
poked the fire and at the instant the apple tree disappeared and

les pommes rouges aussi, et la neige et la glace
the apples red also and the snow and the ice

étaient là comme avant.
were there like before

La   petite   fille   retourna   à   la   maison,   elle   frappa   à   la
The   little   girl   turned back   to   the   house   she   knocked   at   the

porte.   La   mère   ouvrit   la   porte,   et   demanda: "Avez-vous
door   The   mother   opened   the   door   and   asked   Have you

les   neuf   pommes?"
the   nine   apples

"Oui,   ma   mère,"   répondit   la   petite   fille.   Elle   donna   les
Yes   my   mother   answered   the   little   girl   She   gave   the

pommes   à   sa   mère   et   entra   dans   la   maison.
apples   to   her   mother   and   entered   in   the   house

La   mère   donna   les   pommes   à   la   méchante   fille.   La
The   mother   gave   the   apples   to   the   malicious   girl   The

méchante   fille   mangea   les   neuf   pommes,   et   demanda
malicious   girl   ate   the   nine   apples   and   asked

à   Laura: "Ma   soeur,   où   avez-vous   trouvé   ces   grosses
of   Laura   My   sister   where have you   found   these   big

pommes   rouges?"
apples   red

"Dans   la   forêt,   il   y   avait   un   grand   pommier   tout
In   the   forest   it   there had   a   large   apple tree   totally
                         ()   (was)

couvert   de   pommes   rouges,"   répondit   Laura.
covered   with   apples   red   answered   Laura

La	méchante	fille	dit	à	sa	mère	le	lendemain:	"Ma
The	malicious	girl	said	to	her	mother	the	following day	My

mère,	donnez-moi	mon	manteau	et	mon	capuchon.	Je
mother	give me	my	coat	and	my	cap	I

vais	à	la	forêt	cueillir	beaucoup	de	violettes,	de
go	to	the	forest	to pick	many	of	violets	of
						()		()

fraises,	et	de	pommes."
strawberries	and	of	apples
		()	

La	mère	donna	le	manteau	et	le	capuchon	à	Claire,
The	mother	gave	the	coat	and	the	cap	to	Claire

qui	partit.
who	left

Elle	alla	dans	la	forêt,	elle	vit	de	la	glace	et	de
She	went	in	the	forest	she	saw	of	the	ice	and	of
							()	()			()

la	neige,	mais	elle	ne	vit	pas	de	violettes.
the	snow	but	she	not	saw	not	of	violets
()					()	(no)	()	

Elle	ne	vit	pas	de	fraises,	et	elle	ne	vit	pas	de
She	not	saw	not	of	strawberries	and	she	not	saw	not	of
	()		(no)	()				()		(no)	()

pommes.
apples

Elle	chercha	à	droite,	elle	chercha	à	gauche,	en	vain.
She	sought	to	right	she	sought	to	left	in	vain

Alors | elle | dit: | "J'ai | froid, | où | y a-t-il | du | feu?"
Then | she | said | I have (am) | cold | where | there has it (is there) () | of the | fire

Elle | regarda | à | droite | et | à | gauche, | et | vit | le | grand
She | looked | to | right (the right) | and | to | left (the left) | and | saw | the | large

feu | et | les | douze | hommes, | assis | en | silence | autour | du
fire | and | the | twelve | men | sitting | in | silence | around | the

feu.
fire

Claire | s'approcha, | et | l'homme | qui | avait | le | bâton | dit:
Claire | herself approached (approached) | and | the man | who | had | the | staff | said

"Mon | enfant, | que | cherchez-vous | dans | la | forêt | dans
My | child | what | seek you | in | the | forest | in

cette | saison?"
this | season

"Rien," | dit | la | méchante | fille, | qui | était | aussi | très | impolie.
Nothing | said | the | malicious | girl | who | was | also | very | impolite

Frère | Janvier | prit | son | bâton, | attisa | le | feu, | et | dans
Brother | January | took | his | staff | poked | the | fire | and | in

un | instant | la | neige | commença | à | tomber.
an | instant | the | snow | started | with to fall ()

La méchante fille partit pour aller à la maison, mais
The malicious girl left for to go to the house but

en route elle tomba dans la neige et périt.
on way she fell in the snow and perished
(the way)

La mère dit: "Où est Claire?"
The mother said Where is Claire

Un moment après la mère prit son manteau et son
One moment after the mother took her coat and her

capuchon et partit pour chercher Claire.
cap and left for to seek Claire

Elle chercha dans la forêt, elle arriva aussi au grand
She sought in the forest she arrived also at the large

feu et vit les douze hommes.
fire and saw the twelve men

Frère Janvier dit: "Ma bonne femme, que cherchez-vous
Brother January said My good woman what seek you

dans la forêt dans cette saison?" "Rien," répondit la
in the forest in this season Nothing answered the

mère, qui était aussi impolie.
mother who was also impolite

Frère Janvier prit son bâton, attisa le feu, et
Brother January took his staff poked the fire and

à l'instant la neige commença à tomber.
at the instant the snow started to fall

La mère partit pour aller à la maison, mais en route
The mother left for to go to the house but on way
(the way)

elle tomba dans la neige et périt aussi.
she fell in the snow and perished also

La bonne fille était seule dans la maison, mais douze
The good girl was alone in the house but twelve

fois par an elle recevait la visite d'un des douze
times per year she received the visit of one of the twelve

hommes. Décembre, Janvier, et Février apportaient de la
men December January and February brought of the
( ) ( )

glace et de la neige; Mars, Avril, et Mai apportaient
ice and of the snow March April and May brought
( ) ( )

des violettes; Juin, Juillet, et Août apportaient de petits
of the violets June July and August brought of small
( ) ( )

fruits; et Septembre, Octobre, et Novembre apportaient
fruits and September October and November brought

beaucoup de pommes.
many of apples
( )

115 Les Quatre Saisons

La **petite** **fille** **était** **toujours** **très** **polie,** **et** **les** **douze**
The little girl was always ' very polite and the twelve

mois **étaient** **ses** **bons** **amis.**
months were her good friends

.

LES TROIS CITRONS
THE THREE LEMONS

Il y avait une fois un prince beau comme le jour,
It there had one time a prince beautiful like the day
(There was)

riche et aimable. Le roi, son père, désirait beaucoup
rich and pleasant The king his father desired much

de le voir marié, et tous les jours il lui disait: "Mon
to him see married and all the days him he said My

fils, pourquoi ne choisissez-vous pas une femme parmi
son why not choose yourself not a wife among
()

toutes les belles demoiselles de la cour?"
all the beautiful young ladies of the court

Mais le fils regardait toutes les demoiselles avec
But the son looked at all the young ladies with

indifférence, et refusait toujours de choisir une femme.
indifference and refused always to choose a wife

Enfin, un jour, fatigué des remontrances de son père,
Finally one day tired of the remonstrances of his father
(admonitions)

il dit:
he said

"Mon   père,   vous   désirez   me   voir   marié.   Je   n'aime
My   father   you   wish   me   to see   married   I   not like

pas   les   demoiselles   de   la   cour.   Elles   ne   sont   pas
not   the   young ladies   of   the   court   They   not   are   not
()   ()

assez   jolies   pour   me   plaire.   Je   propose   de   faire   un
enough   pretty   for   me   to like   I   propose   to   make   a

long   voyage,   tout   autour   du   monde,   si   c'est   nécessaire,
long   journey   all   around   the   world   if   it is   necessary

et   quand   je   trouverai   une   princesse,   aussi   blanche   que
and   when   I   will find   a   princess   just as   white   as

la   neige,   aussi   belle   que   le   jour,   et   aussi   intelligente
the   snow   just as   beautiful   as   the   day   and   just as   intelligent

et   aimable   qu'un   ange,   je   la   prendrai   pour   femme,
and   pleasant   as an   angel   I   her   will take   as   (a) wife
                                                        (for)

sans   hésiter."
without   to hesitate

Le   roi   était   enchanté   de   cette   décision,   dit   adieu   à
The   king   was   enchanted   of   this   decision   said   good-bye   to

son   fils,   lui   souhaita   un   bon   voyage,   et   le   prince
his   son   him   wished   a   good   journey   and   the   prince

partit   tout   joyeux.
left   all   happy

Il commença son voyage gaiement, et alla tout droit
He started his journey merrily and went all straight

devant lui. Enfin il arriva à la mer, où il trouva un
ahead of him Finally he arrived at the sea where he found a

beau vaisseau à l'ancre.
beautiful vessel at the anchor

Il s'embarqua sur ce vaisseau, et quelques minutes
He embarked on this vessel and some minutes

après des mains mystérieuses et invisibles levèrent
afterwards of the hands mysterious and invisible raised
()

l'ancre, et le vaisseau quitta rapidement le port.
the anchor and the vessel left quickly the port

Le prince navigua ainsi pendant trois jours.
The prince sailed so during three days

Alors le vaisseau arriva à une île.
Then the vessel arrived at an island

Le   prince   débarqua   avec   son   cheval,   et   continua   son
The   prince   disembarked   with   his   horse   and   continued   his

voyage,   malgré   le   froid   intense   et   la   neige   et   la
journey   in spite of   the   cold   intense   and   the   snow   and   the

glace   qui   l'entouraient   de   tous   côtés.   Le   prince   était
ice   which   him surrounded   at   all   sides   The   prince   was

surpris   de   se   trouver   déjà   en   hiver,   mais   il   continua
surprised   to   himself find   already   in   winter   but   he   continued

bravement   son   chemin.
bravely   his   way

Il   arriva   enfin   à   une   toute   petite   maison   blanche.   Il
He   arrived   finally   at   a   very   small   house   white   He

frappa   à   la   porte,   et   une   vieille   dame,   aux   cheveux
knocked   at   the   door   and   an   old   lady   to the   hairs
                                                                    (with)   (hair)

blancs,   ouvrit   la   porte.
white   opened   the   door

"Que   cherchez-vous,   jeune   homme?"   demanda-t-elle.
What   seek you   young   man   asked she

"Je cherche une femme, la plus jolie au monde;
I seek a wife the most pretty in the world

pouvez-vous me dire où la trouver?" répondit le prince.
can you me say where her to find answered the prince

"Non, il n'y a pas de femme pour vous dans mon
No it not there has no of wife for you in my
() (there) (is) ()

royaume. Je suis l'Hiver, je n'ai pas le temps de
kingdom I am the Winter I not have not the time of
(have) (to)

m'occuper de mariages. Mais allez visiter ma soeur,
occupy myself of marriages But go visit my sister
(with)

l'Automne, elle vous trouvera peut-être la femme idéale
the Autumn she you will find maybe the wife ideal

que vous cherchez." Le prince remercia la belle dame
that you seek The prince thanked the beautiful lady

aux cheveux blancs, remonta à cheval, continua son
to the hairs white mounted on horse continued his
(with) (hair) ()

chemin et remarqua bientôt que la neige et la glace
way and noted soon that the snow and the ice

avaient disparu, et que les arbres étaient tout couverts
had disappeared and that the trees were all covered

de beaux fruits.
of beautiful fruits
(with)

Il   arriva   bientôt   après   à   une   petite   maison   brune,   et
He   arrived   soon   after   at   a   small   house   brown   and

frappa   à   la   porte.
knocked   at   the   door

Une   belle   dame,   aux   yeux   et   aux   cheveux   noirs,
A   beautiful   lady   to the   eyes   and   to the   hairs   black
                            (with)   (with)   (hair)

ouvrit   la   porte,   et   demanda   d'une   voix   bien   douce:
opened   the   door   and   asked   of a   voice   very   soft
                                             (with a)

"Que   voulez-vous,   jeune   homme,   et   que   cherchez-vous
What   want you   young   man   and   what   seek you

ici   dans   mon   royaume?"
here   in   my   kingdom

"Je   cherche   une   femme,"   répondit   le   prince   sans
I   seek   a   wife   answered   the   prince   without

hésitation.
hesitation

"Une   femme!"   répéta   la   belle   dame   avec   surprise.
A   wife   repeated   the   beautiful   lady   with   surprise

"Je   n'ai   pas   de   femme   pour   vous.   Je   suis   l'Automne,
I   not have not   of   wife   for   you   I   am   the Autumn
      (have) (no) ()

et   je   suis   très   occupée,   je   vous   assure,   car   j'ai   tous
and   I   am   very   busy   I   you   assure   because I have all

les   fruits   à   cueillir.   Allez   faire   visite   à   ma   soeur,
the   fruits   to   gather   Go   make   visit   to   my   sister
                                              (a visit)

l'Été,   elle   aura   peut-être   le   temps   de   s'occuper   de
the Summer she will have maybe   the   time   to   occupy herself of
                                                                        (with)

vous   et   de   vous   trouver   une   jolie   femme."   Le   prince,
you   and   of   you   find   a   pretty wife   The   prince
             (to)

ainsi   congédié,   continua   son   voyage.   Il   remarqua   avant
thus   dismissed   continued   his   journey   He   noted   before

bien   longtemps   que   l'herbe   était   haute,   que   le   feuillage
very   long time   that   the grass was   high   that the foliage

était   épais,   et   que   le   blé   était   mûr.   Il   n'avait   plus
was   thick   and that the grain was   ripe   He   not had   anymore
                                                            (did not feel)

froid,   au   contraire   il   avait   bien   chaud,   et   il   fut   très
cold   on the contrary   he   had   very   warm   and he   was   very
                                (was)

content   d'apercevoir   une   petite   maison   jaune,   à   peu   de
satisfied to see   a   small   house   yellow   at   little of
                                                                    ()

distance.
distance

Arrivé à la porte de cette petite maison, il heurta, et
Arrived at the door of this small house he knocked and

une jolie femme, aux cheveux bruns et aux joues
a pretty woman to the (with) hairs (hair) brown and to the (with) cheeks

rouges, ouvrit la porte en demandant:
red opened the door while asking

"Que voulez-vous, jeune homme, et que cherchez-vous
What want you young man and what seek you

dans mon royaume?"
in my kingdom

"Madame," dit le prince avec la plus grande politesse,
Madam said the prince with the most large (greatest) courtesy

"j'ai eu l'honneur de faire visite à vos deux soeurs,
I have had the honor to make visit (a visit) to your two sisters

l'Hiver et l'Automne. Je leur ai demandé de me
the Winter and the Autumn I them have asked of (to) me

trouver une femme, la plus jolie du monde, mais elles
find a wife the most pretty of the world but they

sont trop occupées et m'ont envoyé chez vous."
are too busy and have me sent to you

"Pouvez-vous   me   procurer   la   femme   charmante   que   je
Can you   me   acquire   the wife   charming   that I

cherche   depuis   si   longtemps   en   vain?"
seek   since   such   a long time   in   vain

"Ah,   mon   prince,"   répondit   la   belle   dame   aux   cheveux
Ah   my   prince   answered   the beautiful   lady   with the   hairs
                                                                      (hair)

bruns   et   aux   joues   rouges.
brown   and   with the   cheeks   red

"Je   suis   aussi   fort   occupée,   et   je   n'ai   pas   le   temps
I   am   also   extremely   busy   and   I   not have   not   the   time
                                                                              ()

de   vous   trouver   une   femme.   Mais   allez   faire   visite   à
to   you   find   a   wife   But   go   make   visit   with

ma   soeur,   le   Printemps,   elle   vous   aidera   certainement."
my   sister   the   Spring   she   you   will help   certainly

Le   prince   la   remercia   et   partit.
The   prince   her   thanked   and   left

Quelques minutes après il remarqua que l'herbe était
Some minutes afterwards he noted that the grass was

d'un vert plus tendre, que tous les arbres étaient
of a green more tender that all the trees were

couverts de fleurs, et vit une petite maison verte, au
covered with flowers and saw a small house green in the

milieu d'un jardin, où il y avait une grande quantité
middle of a garden where it there had a large quantity
() (was)

de belles fleurs: des tulipes, des jacinthes, des
of beautiful flowers of the tulips of the hyacinths of the
() () ()

jonquilles, des violettes, des lilas, des muguets, etc., etc.
daffodils of the violets of the lilacs of the lilies of the valley etc etc
() () ()

Notre héros heurta à la porte de cette petite maison,
Our hero knocked at the door of this small house

et une dame aux cheveux blonds et aux yeux bleus
and a lady at the hairs fair and with the eyes blue
(with) (hair) (with)

parut immédiatement. "Que cherchez-vous, jeune homme,"
appeared immediately What seek you young man

demanda-t-elle?
asked she

"Je cherche une femme. Vos trois soeurs, l'Hiver,
I seek a wife Your three sisters the Winter

l'Automne et l'Été étaient trop affairées pour
the Autumn and the Summer were too busy for
(to)

m'en procurer une, mais j'espère bien que vous aurez
me of it obtain one but I hope very much that you will have
(obtain for me)

compassion de moi, et que vous me trouverez la
compassion with me and that you me will find the
(for me)

personne charmante que je cherche depuis si longtemps
person charming that I seek since such a long time

en vain."
in vain

"Oui, mon prince, je vous aiderai," répondit la jolie
Yes my prince I you will help answered the pretty

jeune femme. "Entrez dans ma petite maison,
young woman Enter in my small house

asseyez-vous là, à cette petite table, et je vous
seat yourself there at that small table and I you

donnerai à boire et à manger, car vous avez sans
will give to drink and to eat because you have without
(are)

doute bien faim et bien soif."
doubt very hunger and very thirst
(hungry) (thirsty)

Le prince accepta cette invitation, entra, s'assit à table
The prince accepted this invitation entered sat down at table
(the table)

et mangea et but avec plaisir.
and ate and drank with pleasure

Quand il eut fini son repas, le Printemps lui apporta
When he had finished his meal the Spring him brought

trois beaux citrons, un joli couteau d'argent et une
three beautiful lemons a pretty knife of silver and a

magnifique coupe d'or, et dit:
splendid cup of gold and said

"Prince, voici trois citrons, un couteau d'argent et une
Prince here three lemons a knife of silver and a

coupe d'or. Je vous donne ces objets magiques.
cup of gold I you give these objects magic

Quand vous arriverez tout près du château de votre
When you will arrive very near of the castle of your
(of the)

père, arrêtez-vous à la fontaine."
father halt yourself at the fountain

"Prenez   ce   couteau   d'argent,   coupez   le   premier   citron,
Take   this   knife   of silver   cut   the   first   lemon

et   au   même   instant   une   belle   princesse   paraîtra.   Elle
and   at the   same   moment   a   beautiful   princess   will appear   She

vous   demandera   à   boire.   Si   vous   lui   donnez
you   will ask   to   drink   If   you   her   give

immédiatement   à   boire   dans   la   coupe   d'or,   elle   restera
immediately   to   drink   in   the   cup   of gold   she   will remain
                              (from)

avec   vous   et   sera   votre   femme;   mais   si   vous   hésitez,
with   you   and   will be   your   wife   but   if   you   hesitate

même   un   instant,   elle   disparaîtra,   et   vous   ne   la
even   a   moment   she   will disappear   and   you   not   her

reverrez   plus   jamais."
will see again   anymore   never
                              (ever)

"Si   vous   avez   le   malheur   de   la   perdre,   coupez   le
If   you   have   the   misfortune   to   her   lose   cut   the

second   citron,   et   une   seconde   princesse   paraîtra,   qui
second   lemon   and   a   second   princess   will appear   who

vous   demandera   aussi   à   boire.   Si   vous   ne   lui   donnez
you   will ask   also   to   drink   If   you   not   her   give
                                                         ()

pas   immédiatement   à   boire,   elle   disparaîtra   aussi."
not   immediately   to   drink   she   will disappear   also

"Alors vous couperez le troisième citron, une troisième
Then you will cut the third lemon a third

princesse paraîtra; elle demandera à boire, et si vous
princess will appear she will ask to drink and if you

lui permettez de disparaître, aussi, vous n'aurez jamais
her allow to disappear also you will not have never

de femme, et vous n'en mériterez pas, parce que vous
of woman and you not it will deserve not because you
() (a woman) ()

aurez été trop stupide."
will have been too stupid

Le prince écouta les instructions de la jolie dame
The prince listened to the instructions of the pretty lady

avec beaucoup d'attention.
with a lot of attention

Il prit le couteau d'argent, la coupe d'or et les trois
he took the knife of silver the cup of gold and the three

citrons, monta à cheval, et partit.
lemons mounted on horse and left
(on his)

Il passa à travers le royaume du Printemps, de l'Été,
He passed through the kingdom of the Spring of the Summer

de l'Automne, de l'Hiver, arriva au bord de la mer,
of the Autumn of the Winter arrived at the edge of the sea

trouva le vaisseau, s'embarqua, et arriva au bout de
found the vessel embarked and arrived at the end of

trois jours, au port où il s'était embarqué.
three days at the port where he was embarked
(had)

Quelques jours après il arriva à la fontaine près du
Some days afterwards he arrived at the fountain near the

château de son père.
castle of his father

Il descendit de cheval, prit les trois citrons et le
He came down from horse took the three lemons and the
(the horse)

couteau d'argent, remplit la coupe d'or d'eau pure à
knife of silver filled the cup of gold with water pure at

la fontaine, et quand ces préparatifs furent tous finis il
the fountain and when these preparations were all ready he

coupa le premier citron d'une main tremblante.
cut the first lemon of a hand trembling
(with a)

Au   même   instant   une   princesse,   belle   comme   le   jour,
At the   same   moment   a   princess   beautiful   like   the   day

se   présenta   devant   lui,   et   dit   timidement:
herself   presented   in front of   him   and   said   timidly

"Prince,   j'ai   soif,   voulez-vous,   s'il-vous-plaît,   me   donner   à
Prince   I have   thirst   will you   if it pleases you   me   to give   to
        (I am)   (thirsty)   (please)

boire?"
drink

Mais   le   prince   était   si   occupé   à   l'admirer,   qu'il   oublia
But   the   prince   was   so   occupied   with her to admire   that he   forgot

la   recommandation   du   Printemps,   et   ne   lui   donna   pas
the   advise   of the   Spring   and   not   her   gave   not
                                                ()

à   boire.
to   drink

La   princesse   le   regarda   un   instant   d'un   air   de
The   princess   him   looked at   one   moment   with an   expression   of

reproche,   et   puis   elle   disparut.   Le   prince,   au   désespoir,
reproach   and   then   she   disappeared   The   prince   with   despair

pleura   et   se   lamenta.
cried   and   himself   deplored

Il dit cent fois, au moins, qu'il était bien stupide de
He said (a) hundred times at the least that he was very stupid to

laisser échapper une si belle princesse, et enfin il
let escape a so beautiful princess and finally he

se décida à couper le second citron.
decided to cut the second lemon

Une seconde princesse, plus belle que la première, se
A second princess more beautiful than the first herself

présenta aussitôt, et dit: "Prince, j'ai soif, donnez-moi à
presented at once and said Prince I have thirst give me to
(I am) (thirsty)

boire, s'il-vous-plaît."
drink if it pleases you
(please)

Mais le pauvre prince était si surpris de sa beauté,
But the poor prince was so surprised of her beauty

qu'il resta là, la bouche ouverte, et oublia de lui
that he remained there the mouth opened and forgot to her

donner à boire. La seconde princesse le regarda d'un
give to drink The second princess him looked at with a

air de reproche, et disparut aussi.
look of reproach and disappeared also

Alors   le   prince   pleura   et   se   lamenta,   et   dit   au   moins
Then   the   prince   cried   and   himself deplored   and   said   at   least

deux   cents   fois: "Je   suis   stupide,   très   stupide,"   mais
two   hundred   times   I   am   stupid   very   stupid   but

la   princesse   avait   complètement   disparu.
the   princess   had   completely   disappeared

Après   avoir   pleuré   longtemps,   le   prince   se   décida   à
After   to have   cried   a long time   the   prince   himself   decided   to

couper   le   troisième   citron,   et   une   troisième   princesse,
cut   the   third   lemon,   and   a   third   princess

plus   belle   que   les   deux   autres,   se   présenta   devant
more   beautiful   than   the   two   others   herself   presented   in front of

lui: "Prince,"   dit-elle,   timidement,   "j'ai   soif,   donnez-moi   à
him   Prince   said she   timidly   I have   thirst   give me   to
                                                    (I am)   (thirsty)

boire,   s'il-vous-plaît."
drink   if it pleases you
         (please)

Le   prince   lui   donna   à   boire   immédiatement.
The   prince   her   gave   to   drink   immediately

Alors la princesse s'assit à côté de lui, et quand il
Then the princess sat down at side of him and when he

lui demanda si elle voulait bien être sa femme, elle
her asked if she wanted well to be his wife she

rougit, et dit, "Oui."
reddens and said Yes

Le prince la regarda avec admiration, et dit: "Que
The prince her looked at with admiration and said What

vous êtes belle! Vous êtes la plus belle personne du
you are beautiful You are the most beautiful person of the

monde, j'en suis sûr! Mais votre robe n'est pas belle.
world I of it am sure But your dress is not not beautiful
()

Elle est trop modeste. Attendez ici, et j'irai au
It is too modest Wait here and I will go to the

château de mon père, chercher une belle robe de
castle of my father to search a beautiful dress of

satin blanc et une voiture pour vous présenter à mon
satin white and a carriage to you present to my

père comme une grande dame."
father as a great lady

La princesse était très timide; elle avait peur de
The princess was very shy she had fear to
(was) (afraid)

rester seule, mais enfin elle consentit à rester près
stay alone but finally she agreed to stay near

de la fontaine, et le prince partit. Il alla au château
to the fountain and the prince left He went to the castle

de son père, dit qu'il avait trouvé une princesse,
of his father said that he had found a princess

blanche comme la neige, belle comme le jour, et
white as the snow beautiful as the day and

aimable et intelligente comme un ange, et promit de
pleasant and intelligent like an angel and promised to

la présenter dans une heure. Alors le prince alla
her present in an hour Then the prince went

demander une belle robe de satin blanc à sa soeur
to ask a beautiful dress of satin white to his sister
(from)

favorite, donna ordre de préparer la plus belle voiture,
favorite gave order to prepare the most beautiful carriage

et fit tous les préparatifs nécessaires pour recevoir la
and made all the preparations necessary to receive the

princesse avec honneur.
princess with honor

Quand tout fut prêt, il monta en voiture pour aller
When all was ready he got up into (the) carriage to go

chercher la belle princesse qu'il était impatient de revoir.
seek the beautiful princess that he was impatient to see again

Pendant son absence, la princesse, qui avait peur de
During his absence the princess who had fear to
(was) (afraid)

rester là toute seule, grimpa dans un grand arbre,
remain there all alone climbed in a large tree

près de la fontaine, et se cacha dans le feuillage.
near of the fountain and herself hid in the foliage

Tout son corps était complètement caché, mais sa jolie
All of her body was completely hidden but her pretty

figure était visible, et se reflétait dans l'eau pure de
figure was visible and itself reflected in the water pure of

la fontaine, comme dans un miroir.
the fountain like in a mirror

Quelques minutes après, une servante arriva à la
Some minutes afterwards a servant girl arrived at the

fontaine pour chercher de l'eau.
fountain to seek of the water
() (water)

Elle avait une grande cruche, elle se pencha sur
She had a large jug she herself leaned over

l'eau, vit la jolie figure, et regarda à droite et à
the water saw the pretty figure and looked to right and to
(the right)

gauche pour découvrir la personne à qui cette jolie
left to discover the person to whom this pretty
(the left)

figure appartenait.
figure belonged

Mais elle ne vit personne, et décida bientôt que
But she not saw nobody and decided soon that
()

l'image qu'elle voyait dans l'eau était celle de sa
the image that she saw in the water was that of her

propre figure: "Oh, que je suis jolie," dit-elle avec joie.
own figure Oh what I am pretty said she with joy
(how)

"Que je suis jolie. Je suis aussi jolie qu'une
What I am pretty I am so pretty as a

princesse. Ma maîtresse dit toujours: 'Lucie, vous êtes
princess My mistress says always Lucie you are

laide, laide à faire peur,' mais ce n'est pas vrai. Je
ugly ugly to make afraid but this is not not true I
() ()

suis jolie, et ma maîtresse est jalouse parce que je
am pretty and my mistress is jealous because I

suis plus jolie qu'elle. Je suis trop jolie pour porter
am more pretty than she I am too pretty to carry

de l'eau!" Et la servante cassa sa cruche sur les
of the water And the servant girl broke her jug on the
() (water)

pierres, et retourna chez sa maîtresse, qui attendait
stones and turned back to her mistress who awaited

l'eau avec impatience.
the water with impatience

"Où est la cruche?" demanda-t-elle. "Où est l'eau que
Where is the jug asked she Where is the water that

je vous ai dit de m'apporter?"
I you have said to bring to me

"J'ai cassé la cruche, je suis trop jolie pour porter
I have broken the jug I am too pretty to carry

de l'eau," dit la servante.
of the water said the servant girl
() (water)

"Vous! Jolie!" dit la dame avec étonnement, "vous êtes
You Pretty said the lady with astonishment you are

laide à faire peur!" Et la maîtresse, en colère, battit
ugly to make fear And the mistress in anger beat

la pauvre servante, lui donna une autre cruche, et la
the poor servant girl her gave another jug and her

renvoya en pleurant à la fontaine.
sent back crying to the fountain

La servante retourna lentement à la fontaine, se pencha
The servant girl turned back slowly to the fountain leaned

sur l'eau, vit la même jolie figure, et dit: "Oh, que
over the water saw the same pretty figure and said Oh what

je suis jolie! Je suis sûre que je suis la plus jolie
I am pretty I am sure that I am the most pretty

personne du monde!"
person of the world

"Je ne porterai pas l'eau pour ma maîtresse," et elle
I not will carry not the water for my mistress and she
(no) (water)

cassa la seconde cruche et retourna à la maison
broke the second jug and turned back to the house

sans eau.
without water

"Où est l'eau de la fontaine, esclave?" demanda la
Where is the water of the fountain slave asked the

maîtresse impérieusement.
mistress imperiously

"L'eau est dans la fontaine, et la cruche est cassée.
The water is in the fountain and the jug is broken

Je ne serai plus votre servante. Je suis trop jolie.
I not will be anymore your maidservant I am too pretty

Je suis assez jolie pour épouser le prince."
I am enough pretty to marry the prince

Alors la maîtresse commença à rire, et dit:
Then the mistress started to laugh and said

"Que vous êtes absurde, Lucie; vous êtes laide, laide
What you are absurd Lucie you are ugly ugly
(how)

à faire peur; retournez à la fontaine!"
to make afraid go back to the fountain

La servante retourna à la fontaine avec une troisième
The servant girl returned to the fountain with a third

cruche et se pencha sur l'eau. Quand elle vit la jolie
jug and leaned over the water When she saw the pretty

figure, réfléchie dans l'eau limpide, elle dit: "Oh, que
figure reflected in the water clear she said Oh what

je suis jolie!" et cette fois elle parla si haut que la
I am pretty and this time she spoke so loud that the

princesse dans l'arbre l'entendit.
princess in the tree it heard

Amusée par ces exclamations, elle se mit à rire. La
Amused by these exclamations she herself put to laugh The
(started)

servante, surprise, leva la tête, et vit la jolie
servant girl surprised raised the head and saw the pretty

princesse:
princess

"Ah,"   pensa-t-elle,   "c'est   cette   personne-là   qui   a   causé
Ah   thought she   it is   this   person there   who   has caused

tout   mon   malheur!   Je   me   vengerai!"   Alors   d'une   voix
all   my   misfortune I   me   will avenge Then   with a voice

bien   douce,   elle,   dit: "Ma   jolie   dame,   pourquoi
very   sweet   she   said   My   pretty lady   why

êtes-vous   dans   cet   arbre?"
are you   in   that tree

"Pour   attendre   le   prince,   mon   fiancé,   qui   est   allé   au
To   await   the prince   my   fiancé   who   is   gone   to the

palais   du   roi,   son   père,   chercher   une   belle   robe   de
palace   of the king his   father to search   a   beautiful dress of

satin   blanc,   et   une   voiture."
satin   white   and a   carriage

"Ma   jolie   dame,   vos   beaux   cheveux   blonds   sont   en
My   pretty lady   your beautiful hairs   fair   are   in
                            (hair)   (is)

désordre,   voulez-vous   me   permettre   de   grimper   dans
disorder   will you   me   allow   of   climb   in
                                            (to)

l'arbre   et   de   vous   les   arranger?"
the tree and of   (for) you them arrange
               (to)

La   princesse   consentit,   la   servante   grimpa   sur   l'arbre,
The   princess   agreed   the servant girl climbed in   the tree

prit   une   grande   épingle,   et   perça   la   tête   de   la
took   a   large   hairpin   and pierced the head   of   the

pauvre   princesse,   qui   jeta   un   cri   terrible   et   disparut.
poor   princess   who   emitted a   cry   terrible   and disappeared

La   servante,   surprise,   leva   la   tête   et   vit   un   joli
The   servant girl surprised   raised the head   and saw   a   pretty

pigeon   blanc   qui   s'envolait   en   poussant   des   cris
pigeon   white   who   flew away   emitting   of the cries
                                                     ()

plaintifs.   Alors   la   servante   s'assit   à   la   place   de   la
plaintive   Then   the   servant girl sat down at the place   of   the

princesse   et   attendit   le   retour   du   prince.
princess   and awaited   the return   of the prince

Quelques   minutes   après   le   prince   arriva   avec   toute   sa
Some   minutes   after   the prince   arrived with   all   his

suite.   Il   regarda   à   droite   et   à   gauche,   et   ne   vit
entourage He looked   to right   and to left   and not   saw
                            (the right)   (the left)

personne.
nobody

Il commença à appeler:
He started to call

"Ma princesse, ma belle fiancée, ma bien-aimée, où
My princess my beautiful fiancée my very much beloved where

êtes-vous?"
are you

"Ici," répondit la servante.
Here answered the servant girl

Le prince courut à l'arbre avec empressement. Mais
The prince ran to the tree with eagerness But

quelle ne fut pas sa surprise et son chagrin quand il
what not was not his surprise and his sorrow when he
()

vit la vilaine servante, au lieu de sa charmante fiancée.
saw the unpleasant servant girl in the place of his charming fiancée
(in)

"Où est ma princesse, ma fiancée, une dame belle
Where is my princess my fiancée a lady beautiful

comme le jour et blanche comme la neige?"
like the day and white like the snow
()

demanda-t-il.
asked he

"Je suis votre fiancée," dit la servante; "je suis la
I am your fiancée said the servant girl I am the

belle princesse, je suis votre bien-aimée. Mais pendant
beautiful princess I am your very much beloved But during

votre absence une méchante fée est venue et m'a
your absence a malicious fairy is come and me has
(has)

changée en servante, comme vous voyez." Le prince
changed in servant girl as you see The prince

était un homme d'honneur, et comme il avait demandé
was a man of honor and as he had asked

la main de la jolie princesse, il pensa: "Je suis forcé
the hand of the pretty princess he thought I am forced

d'épouser cette personne, parce qu' elle déclare qu'elle
to marry this person because she declares that she

est ma fiancée."
is my fiancée

Alors il aida la servante à descendre de l'arbre et
Then he helped the servant girl to come down from the tree and

appela les dames d'honneur, qui regardèrent leur
called the ladies of honor who looked at their

nouvelle souveraine avec dégoût.
new sovereign with dislike

Le prince leur ordonna de vêtir la servante, et elles
The prince them ordered to dress the servant girl and they

lui donnèrent la belle robe de satin blanc, le voile
her gave the beautiful dress of satin white the veil

de mariée, et la couronne de fleurs d'oranger. Mais
of marriage and the crown of flowers of orange tree But

toute cette belle toilette la faisait paraître plus laide
all this beautiful toiletry her made to appear more ugly

que jamais.
than never
(ever)

Quand la toilette de la servante fut complètement finie,
When the dressing of the servant girl was completely finished

le prince la conduisit à la voiture, prit place à côté
the prince her led to the carriage took place next

d'elle, et alla au château.
to her and went to the castle

Le vieux roi, anxieux de voir la beauté de sa future
The old king anxious to see the beauty of his future

belle-fille, la reçut à la porte.
daughter in law her received at the door

Il regarda la servante avec surprise, se tourna vers
He looked at the servant girl with surprise turned towards

son fils et dit avec colère:
his son and said with anger

"Mon fils, êtes-vous fou? Vous avez dit que la
My son are you insane You have said that the

princesse que vous aviez choisie était plus blanche
princess that you had chosen was more white

que la neige, plus belle que le jour, intelligente et
than the snow more beautiful than the day intelligent and
()

aimable comme un ange, et maintenant vous arrivez
pleasant like an angel and now you arrive

avec une vilaine servante, qui est laide à faire peur."
with an unpleasant servant girl who is ugly to make fear

Le roi était si en colère contre son fils qu'il lui
The king was so much in anger against his son that he him

tourna le dos, et alla dans sa chambre, où il pleura
turned the back and went in his room where he cried

de rage.
of rage

Le prince conduisit la servante à l'appartement qui
The prince led the servant girl to the apartment that

avait été préparé pour elle.
had been prepared for her

Il plaça le château et tous les domestiques à sa
He placed the castle and all the servants to her

disposition, et lui dit que leur mariage aurait lieu
disposition and he said that their marriage would have place

seulement le lendemain.
only the following day

Alors le prince alla trouver son père, lui raconta
Then the prince went to find his father he told

toutes ses aventures, et déclara qu'il ne se consolerait
all his adventures and declared that he not would be comforted
()

jamais de la perte de la jolie princesse, mais, qu'étant
never of the loss of the pretty princess but that being

un homme d'honneur, il ne pourrait jamais refuser
a man of honor he not could never refuse
()

d'épouser la servante.
to marry the servant girl

Pendant que le prince était avec son père, la
During that the prince was with his father the

servante, heureuse de commander aux autres, alla
servant girl happy to command to the others went
(the)

partout dans le palais, donna des ordres à tous les
everywhere in the palace gave of the orders to all the
()

domestiques, et arriva enfin à la cuisine, où elle dit
servants and arrived finally at the kitchen where she said

au chef de faire beaucoup de bonnes choses à
to the chef to make many of good things to
()

manger.
eat

Pendant qu'elle donnait cet ordre, un joli pigeon blanc
During that she gave this order a pretty pigeon white

vint se poser sur un arbre, tout près de la fenêtre
came to pose herself in a tree all near of the window
(very)

de la cuisine, et poussa un petit cri plaintif.
of the kitchen and emitted a small cry plaintive

La servante vit le pigeon, le montra au chef, et dit:
The servant girl saw the pigeon her showed to the chef and said

"Chef, prenez votre grand couteau, coupez la tête à
Chef take your large knife cut the head of

ce pigeon, et faites-le rôtir pour mon souper."
that pigeon and make it roast for my supper

Le cuisinier prit son grand couteau, alla dans le
The cook took his large knife went in the

jardin, et tua le pauvre petit pigeon blanc.
garden and killed the poor small pigeon white

Trois gouttes de sang tombèrent à terre, et le chef
Three drops of blood fell on earth and the chef

porta le pigeon à la cuisine pour le rôtir pour le
carried the pigeon to the cuisine to it roast for the

souper de la servante, sa nouvelle maîtresse.
supper of the servant girl his new mistress

Le prince avait quitté son père, et il s'était retiré
The prince had left his father and he was withdrawn
(had)

dans sa chambre pour pleurer la belle princesse.
in his room to weep over the beautiful princess

Il était près de la fenêtre; il vit le cuisinier tuer le
He was near of the window he saw the cook kill the

pigeon blanc, et il remarqua les trois gouttes de sang
pigeon white and he noted the three drops of blood

qui tombèrent à terre.
which fell on earth
(the ground)

Quelques minutes après que le cuisinier fut parti, le
Some minutes after that the cook was left the
(had)

prince remarqua trois petites plantes qui sortaient de
prince noted three small plants that came out of

terre à la place où les trois gouttes de sang du
earth at the place where the three drops of blood of the
(the earth)

pigeon étaient tombées. Ces trois petites plantes
pigeon were fallen These three small plants
(had)

poussaient avec une rapidité extraordinaire, et en
pushed with a speed extraordinary and in
(grew)

quelques minutes le prince vit avec surprise trois
some minutes the prince saw with surprise three
(a few)

arbres, tout couverts de fleurs.
trees all covered of flowers
(with)

Quelques minutes après les fleurs avaient disparu, et
Some minutes afterwards the flowers had disappeared and

le prince remarqua trois fruits verts.
the prince noted three fruits green

En un instant les fruits étaient mûrs, et le prince vit
In a moment the fruits were ripe and the prince saw

avec surprise que ces fruits étaient trois citrons.
with surprise that these fruits were three lemons

Il descendit dans le jardin, cueillit les trois citrons,
He went down in the garden picked the three lemons
              (into)

remonta dans sa chambre, remplit la coupe d'or d'eau
went up in his room filled the cup of gold with water
         (into)

fraîche, et prit le couteau d'argent. Le pauvre prince
fresh and took the knife of silver The poor prince

coupa le premier citron, en tremblant; la première
cut the first lemon trembling the first

princesse parut, et demanda à boire, mais le prince
princess appeared and asked to drink but the prince

dit:
said

"Oh non, charmante princesse, ce n'est pas vous que
Oh no   charming princess it is not not you that
()

je veux pour femme."
I want for wife

Il coupa le second citron, la seconde princesse parut,
He cut the second lemon the second princess appeared

et il lui refusa aussi à boire. Mais quand il coupa
and he her refused also to drink But when he cut
(give to drink)

le troisième citron et que la troisième princesse parut,
the third lemon and that the third princess appeared
(when)

il lui donna à boire avec empressement, et elle resta
he her gave to drink with eagerness and she stayed

avec lui, et il l'embrassa avec joie. La jolie princesse
with him and he embraced her with joy The pretty princess

raconta toutes ses aventures au prince, et il dit que
told all her adventures to the prince and he said that

la servante serait punie. Mais le prince était si
the servant girl would be punished But the prince was so

heureux de revoir sa chère princesse qu'il dansa de
happy to see again his dear princess that he danced of

joie.
joy

Le roi, entendant le bruit dans la chambre du prince,
The king hearing the noise in the room of the prince

arriva en colère, ouvrit la porte, et dit: "Mon fils,
arrived in anger opened the door and said My son

vous êtes décidément fou! Pourquoi dansez-vous
you are definitely insane Why dance you

maintenant?" "Oh mon père," répondit le prince, "je
now Oh my father answered the prince I

danse de joie, parce que j'ai retrouvé la chère
dance of joy because I have found again the dear

princesse, la plus jolie femme du monde!" et le prince
princess the most pretty woman of the world and the prince

présenta la princesse à son père, qui la regarda avec
presented the princess to his father who her regarded with

admiration, et dit: "Mon fils, vous avez raison, cette
admiration and said My son you have reason this
have reason
(are) (right)

princesse est belle comme le jour, blanche comme la
princess is beautiful like the day white like the

neige, et je suis sûr qu'elle est aussi bonne et
snow and I am sure that she is also good and

intelligente qu'un ange!"
intelligent as an angel

Alors le roi demanda au prince comment il avait
Then the king asked of the prince how he had

retrouvé la princesse, où elle avait disparu, et quand
found back the princess where she had disappeared and when

il eut entendu toute l'histoire, il dit:
he had heard all the history he said

"La servante est une très méchante femme. Elle mérite
The servant girl is a very malicious woman She deserves

une punition très sévère."
a punishment very severe

Alors le roi prit un grand voile, le jeta sur la tête
Then the king took a large veil it threw on the head

de la princesse, et la mena dans la grande salle, où
of the princess and her escorted in the large hall where

tous les courtisans étaient assemblés autour de la
all the courtiers were assembled around of the
()

servante, qui portait une robe de satin rose toute
servant girl who wore a dress of satin pink all

couverte de perles et de diamants.
covered of pearls and of diamonds
(with) (with)

Le roi s'avança vers la servante et dit:
The king advanced towards the servant girl and said

"Madame, demain vous pensez être la reine de ce
Madam tomorrow you think to be the queen of this

royaume. Donnez-moi votre opinion, et dites-moi quelle
kingdom Give me your opinion and tell me which

punition mérite la personne qui attaquerait la future
punishment deserves the person who would attack the future

femme du prince, mon fils?"
wife of the prince my son

"Une personne qui attaquerait la femme de votre fils
A person who would attack the wife of your son

mériterait une mort terrible. Elle mériterait d'être jetée
would deserve a death terrible She would deserve to be thrown

dans un grand four, rôtie toute vive, et je
in a large furnace roasted all alive and I

commanderais que ses cendres fussent jetées au vent."
would order that her ashes were thrown to the wind
(to be)

Le   roi   répondit:
The   king   answered

"Madame,   vous   avez   prononcé   votre   propre   punition.
Madam   you   have   pronounced   your   own   punishment

Vous   êtes   une   femme   cruelle!   Vous   avez   voulu   tuer
You   are   a   woman   cruel   You   have   wanted   to kill

cette   jolie   princesse,   la   future   femme   de   mon   fils,   et
this   pretty   princess   the   future   wife   of   my   son   and

vous   serez   jetée   dans   un   four,   rôtie   toute   vive,   et   je
you   will be   thrown   in   a   furnace   roasted   all   alive   and   I

commanderai   que   vos   cendres   soient   jetées   au   vent!"
will order   that   your   ashes   are   thrown   to the   wind

Alors   le   roi   leva   le   voile   de   la   princesse,   et   tous
Then   the   king   raised   the   veil   of   the   princess   and   all

les   courtisans   et   toutes   les   dames   d'honneur   s'écrièrent:
the   courtiers   and   all   the   ladies   of honor   exclaimed

"Oh,   quelle   jolie   princesse!"
Oh   what   pretty   princess
     (what a)

La pauvre servante se jeta à genoux devant le roi,
The poor servant girl threw herself at knees in front of the king
(the knees)

et dit:
and said

"Mon roi, mon roi, ayez compassion de moi, ayez
My king my king have mercy on me have

compassion de moi, ne me faites pas rôtir toute vive
mercy on me not me make not to roast all alive
()

dans un four. Pardon, mon roi, pardon!"
in a furnace Forgiveness my king forgiveness

Mais le roi refusa de pardonner à la servante; alors
But the king refused to forgive to the servant girl then
()

la belle princesse s'avança, et dit:
the beautiful princess came forward and said

"Votre majesté a promis de me donner un beau
Your majesty has promised of me to give a beautiful
()

cadeau de noces. Donnez-moi la vie de cette pauvre
gift of marriage Give me the life of this poor

créature si ignorante!"
creature so ignorant

Le roi consentit à la demande de la princesse, qui
The king consented to the demand of the princess who

trouva une bonne place pour la servante, et tout le
found a good place for the servant girl and all the

monde déclara que la nouvelle reine était aussi bonne
world declared that the new queen was also good

que belle.
as beautiful

Le mariage du prince et de la princesse fut célébré
The marriage of the prince and of the princess was celebrated

le lendemain avec beaucoup de pompe et de
the following day with much of pump and of
( ) ( )

cérémonie, et le prince et la princesse furent heureux
circumstance and the prince and the princess were happy

tout le reste de leur vie, et regrettés après leur mort
all the rest of their life, and grieved for after their death
(lives)

de tous leurs sujets.
by all their subjects

163   Les Trois Citrons

The book you're now reading contains the paper or digital paper version of the powerful e-book application from Bermuda Word. Our software integrated e-books allow you to become fluent in French reading and listening, fast and easy! Go to <u>learn-to-read-foreign-languages.com</u>, and get the App version of this e-book!

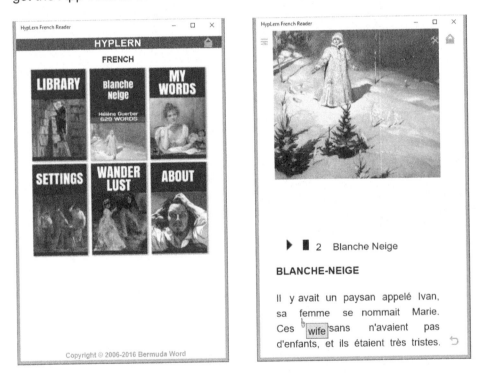

The standalone e-reader software contains the e-book text, includes audio and integrates **spaced repetition word practice** for **optimal language learning**. Choose your font type or size and read as you would with a regular e-reader. Stay immersed with **interlinear** or **immediate mouse-over pop-up translation** and click on difficult words to **add them to your wordlist**. The software knows which words are low frequency and need more practice.

With the Bermuda Word e-book program you **memorize all words** fast and easy just by reading and listening and efficient practice!

LEARN-TO-READ-FOREIGN-LANGUAGES.COM
Contact us using the button on the site!

Made in the USA
Coppell, TX
03 November 2020